OCaml from the Very Beginning

CW00544021

In *OCaml from the Very Beginning* John Whitington takes a no-prerequisites approach to teaching a modern general-purpose programming language. Each small, self-contained chapter introduces a new topic, building until the reader can write quite substantial programs. There are plenty of questions and, crucially, worked answers and hints.

OCaml from the Very Beginning will appeal both to new programmers, and experienced programmers eager to explore functional languages such as OCaml. It is suitable both for formal use within an undergraduate or graduate curriculum, and for the interested amateur.

JOHN WHITINGTON founded a software company which uses OCaml extensively. He teaches functional programming to students of Computer Science at the University of Cambridge.

OCaml

from the very beginning

John Whitington

COHERENT PRESS

C O H E R E N T   P R E S S

Cambridge

Published in the United Kingdom by Coherent Press, Cambridge

© Coherent Press 2013

First published June 2013
Reprinted with corrections October 2013
Reprinted 2014, 2015, 2016, 2017

A catalogue record for this book is available from the British Library

ISBN 978-0-9576711-0-2 Paperback

by the same author

PDF Explained (O'Reilly, 2012)
More OCaml: Algorithms, Methods & Diversions (Coherent, 2014)
A Machine Made this Book: Ten Sketches of Computer Science (Coherent, 2016)

Contents

Preface

This book is based on the Author's experience of teaching programming to students in the University of Cambridge supervisions system. In particular, working with students for the first-year undergraduate course "Foundations of Computer Science", based on Standard ML and lectured for many years by Lawrence C. Paulson.

An interesting aspect of supervising students from a wide range of backgrounds (some with no previous experience at all taking Computer Science as an additional subject within the Cambridge Natural Sciences curriculum, and some with a great deal of programming experience already) is the level playing field which the ML family of languages (like OCaml) provide. Sometimes, those students with least prior programming experience perform the best.

I have tried to write a book which has no prerequisites – and with which any intelligent undergraduate ought to be able to cope, whilst trying to be concise enough that someone coming from another language might not be too annoyed by the tone.

Special note to those who have already written programs

When I was a boy, our class was using a word processor for the first time. I wanted a title for my story, so I typed it on the first line and then, placing the cursor at the beginning, held down the space bar until the title was roughly in the middle. My friend taught me how to use the centring function, but it seemed more complicated to me, and I stuck with the familiar way – after all, it worked. Later on, of course, when I had more confidence and experience, I realized he had been right.

When starting a language which is fundamentally different from those you have seen before, it can be difficult to see the advantages, and to try to think of every concept in terms of the old language. I would urge you to consider the possibility that, at the moment, you might be the boy holding down the space bar.

Acknowledgments

Inevitably, the approach here owes a debt to that taken by Lawrence C. Paulson, both in his lecture notes and in his book "ML for the Working Programmer" (Cambridge University Press, 1996). Question 3 in Chapter 11 is inspired by an examination question of his. I was taught Standard ML by Professor Paulson and Andrei Serjantov in Autumn 2000. Mark Shinwell has been a constant source of helpful discussion. Robin Walker and latterly Andrew Rice have arranged the supervisions system at Queens' College within which I have taught since 2004. I am grateful to the developers of OCaml who have provided such a pleasant environment in which to write programs. Helpful comments on an earlier draft were provided by Martin DeMello, Damien Doligez, Arthur Guillon, Zhi Han, Robert Jakob, Xavier Leroy, Florent Monnier, and Benjamin Pierce. And, of course, I thank all my students, some of whom are now working with OCaml for a living.

Getting Ready

This book is about teaching the computer to do new things by writing *computer programs*. Just as there are different languages for humans to speak to one another, there are different *programming languages* for humans to speak to computers.

We are going to be using a programming language called **OCaml**. It might already be on your computer, or you may have to find it on the internet and install it yourself. You will know that you have OCaml working when you see something like this:

```
        OCaml

#
```

OCaml is waiting for us to type something. Try typing $\boxed{1}$ $\boxed{\text{space}}$ $\boxed{+}$ $\boxed{\text{space}}$ $\boxed{2}$ $\boxed{;}$ $\boxed{;}$ followed by the $\boxed{\text{Enter}}$ key. You should see this:

```
        OCaml

# 1 + 2;;
- : int = 3
```

OCaml is telling us the result of the calculation. To leave OCaml, give the `exit 0` command, again ending with ; ; to tell OCaml we have finished typing:

```
        OCaml

# exit 0;;
```

You should find yourself back where you were before. If you make a mistake when typing, you can press $\boxed{\text{Ctrl-C}}$ (hold down the $\boxed{\text{Ctrl}}$ key and tap the $\boxed{\text{c}}$ key). This will allow you to start again:

```
        OCaml

# 1 + 3^CInterrupted
# 1 + 2;;
- : int = 3
```

We are ready to begin.

Chapter 1

Starting Off

We will cover a fair amount of material in this chapter and its questions, since we will need a solid base on which to build. You should read this with a computer running OCaml in front of you.

Consider first the mathematical expression $1 + 2 \times 3$. What is the result? How did you work it out? We might show the process like this:

$$
\begin{aligned}
& 1 + 2 \times 3 \\
\implies \quad & 1 + 6 \\
\implies \quad & 7
\end{aligned}
$$

How did we know to multiply 2 by 3 first, instead of adding 1 and 2? How did we know when to stop? Let us underline the part of the expression which is dealt with at each step:

$$
\begin{aligned}
& 1 + \underline{2 \times 3} \\
\implies \quad & \underline{1 + 6} \\
\implies \quad & 7
\end{aligned}
$$

We chose which part of the expression to deal with each time using a familiar mathematical rule – multiplication is done before addition. We stopped when the expression could not be processed any further.

Computer programs in OCaml are just like these expressions. In order to give you an answer, the computer needs to know all the rules you know about how to process the expression correctly. In fact, $1 + 2 \times 3$ is a valid OCaml expression as well as a valid mathematical one, but we must write $*$ instead of $\times$, since there is no $\times$ key on the keyboard:

OCaml

```
# 1 + 2 * 3;;
- : int = 7
```

Here, # is OCaml prompting us to write an expression, and `1 + 2 * 3;;` is what we typed (the semicolons followed by the Enter key tell OCaml we have finished our expression). OCaml responds with the answer 7. OCaml also prints int, which tells us that the answer is a whole number, or *integer*.

Let us look at our example expression some more. There are two *operators*: $+$ and $\times$. There are three *operands*: 1, 2, and 3. When we wrote it down, and when we typed it into OCaml, we put spaces between

1

the operators and operands for readability. How does OCaml process it? Firstly, the text we wrote must be split up into its basic parts: 1, +, 2, *, and 3. OCaml then looks at the order and kind of the operators and operands, and decides how to parenthesize the expression: $(1 + (2 \times 3))$. Now, evaluating the expression just requires dealing with each parenthesized section, starting with the innermost, and stopping when there are no parentheses left:

$$
\begin{aligned}
& (1 + \underline{(2 \times 3)}) \\
\implies\quad & \underline{(1 + 6)} \\
\implies\quad & 7
\end{aligned}
$$

OCaml knows that $\times$ is to be done before $+$, and parenthesizes the expression appropriately. We say the $\times$ operator has *higher precedence* than the $+$ operator.

An *expression* is any valid OCaml program. To produce an answer, OCaml *evaluates* the expression, yielding a special kind of expression, a *value*. In our previous example, $1 + 2 \times 3$, $1 + 6$, and 7 were all expressions, but only 7 was a value.

Each expression (and so each value) has a *type*. The type of 7 is **int** (it is an integer). The types of the expressions $1 + 6$ and $1 + 2 \times 3$ are also **int**, since they will evaluate to a value of type **int**. The type of any expression may be worked out by considering the types of its sub-expressions, and how they are combined to form the expression. For example, $1 + 6$ has type **int** because 1 is an **int**, 6 is an **int**, and the $+$ operator takes two integers and gives another one (their sum). Here are the mathematical operators on integers:

Operator	Description
a + b	addition
a - b	subtract b from a
a * b	multiplication
a / b	divide a by b, returning the whole part
a mod b	divide a by b, returning the remainder

The mod, *, and / operators have higher precedence than the + and - operators. For any operator $\oplus$ above, the expression $a \oplus b \oplus c$ is equivalent to $(a \oplus b) \oplus c$ rather than $a \oplus (b \oplus c)$ (we say the operators are *left associative*). We sometimes write down the type of an expression after a colon when working on paper, to keep it in mind:

```
5 * -2 : int
```

(negative numbers are written with - before them). Of course, there are many more types than just **int**. Sometimes, instead of numbers, we would like to talk about truth: either something is true or it is not. For this we use the type **bool** which represents *boolean values*, named after the English mathematician George Boole (1815–1864) who pioneered their use. There are just two things of type **bool**:

```
true
false
```

How can we use these? One way is to use one of the *comparison operators*, which are used for comparing values to one another. For example:

```
OCaml
```

```
# 99 > 100;;
- : bool = false
# 4 + 3 + 2 + 1 = 10;;
- : bool = true
```

Here are all the comparison operators:

Operator	Description
$a = b$	true if a and b are equal
$a < b$	true if a is less than b
$a <= b$	true if a is less than or equal to b
$a > b$	true if a is more than b
$a >= b$	true if a is more than or equal to b
$a <> b$	true if a is not equal to b

Notice that if we try to use operators with types for which they are not intended, OCaml will not accept the program at all, showing us where our mistake is by underlining it:

OCaml

```
# 1 + true;;
Error: This expression has type bool but an expression was expected of type
       int
```

You can find more information about error messages in OCaml in the appendix "Coping with Errors" at the back of this book.

There are two operators for combining boolean values (for instance, those resulting from using the comparison operators). The expression a && b evaluates to true only if a and b both evaluate to true. The expression a || b evaluates to true only if a evaluates to true, b evaluates to true, or both do. The && operator (pronounced "and") is of higher precedence than the || operator (pronounced "or"), so a && b || c is the same as (a && b) || c.

A third type we shall be using is **char** which holds a single *character*, such as 'a' or '?'. We write these in single quotation marks:

OCaml

```
# 'c';;
- : char = 'c'
```

So far we have looked only at operators like +, mod, and = which look like familiar mathematical ones. But many constructs in programming languages look a little different. For example, to choose a course of evaluation based on some test, we use the **if** … **then** … **else** construct:

OCaml

```
# if 100 > 99 then 0 else 1;;
- : int = 0
```

The expression between **if** and **then** (in our example 100 > 99) must have type **bool** – it evaluates to either true or false. The types of the expression to choose if true and the expression to choose if false must be the same as one another – here they are both of type **int**. The whole expression evaluates to the same type – **int** – because either the **then** part or the **else** part is chosen to be the result of evaluating the whole expression:

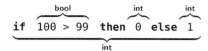

We have covered a lot in this chapter, but we need all these basic tools before we can write interesting programs. Make sure you work through the questions on paper, on the computer, or both, before moving on. Hints and answers are at the back of the book.

Questions

1. What are the types of the following expressions and what do they evaluate to, and why?

   ```
   17
   1 + 2 * 3 + 4
   800 / 80 / 8
   400 > 200
   1 <> 1
   true || false
   true && false
   if true then false else true
   '%'
   'a' + 'b'
   ```

2. Consider the evaluations of the expressions `1 + 2 mod 3`, `(1 + 2) mod 3`, and `1 + (2 mod 3)`. What can you conclude about the `+` and `mod` operators?

3. A programmer writes `1+2 * 3+4`. What does this evaluate to? What advice would you give him?

4. The range of numbers available is limited. There are two special numbers: `min_int` and `max_int`. What are their values on your computer? What happens when you evaluate the expressions `max_int + 1` and `min_int - 1`?

5. What happens when you try to evaluate the expression `1 / 0`? Why?

6. Can you discover what the `mod` operator does when one or both of the operands are negative? What about if the first operand is zero? What if the second is zero?

7. Why not just use, for example, the integer `0` to represent false and the integer `1` for true? Why have a separate **bool** type at all?

8. What is the effect of the comparison operators like < and > on alphabetic values of type **char**? For example, what does `'p' < 'q'` evaluate to? What is the effect of the comparison operators on the booleans, `true` and `false`?

So Far

1 Integers min_int ... -3 -2 -1 0 1 2 3 ... max_int of type **int**. Booleans true and false of type **bool**. Characters of type **char** like 'X' and '!'.

Mathematical operators + - * / mod which take two integers and give another.

Operators = < <= > >= <> which compare two values and evaluate to either true or false.

The conditional **if** *expression1* **then** *expression2* **else** *expression3*, where *expresssion1* has type **bool** and *expression2* and *expression3* have the same type as one another.

The boolean operators && and || which allow us to build compound boolean expressions.

Chapter 2

Names and Functions

So far we have built only tiny toy programs. To build bigger ones, we need to be able to name things so as to refer to them later. We also need to write expressions whose result depends upon one or more other things.

Before, if we wished to use a sub-expression twice or more in a single expression, we had to type it multiple times:

OCaml

```
# 200 * 200 * 200;;
- : int = 8000000
```

Instead, we can define our own name to stand for the result of evaluating an expression, and then use the name as we please:

OCaml

```
# let x = 200;;
val x : int = 200
# x * x * x;;
- : int = 8000000
```

To write this all in a single expression, we can use the **let** ... = ... **in** construct:

OCaml

```
# let x = 200 in x * x * x;;
- : int = 8000000
# let a = 500 in (let b = a * a in a + b);;
- : int = 250500
```

We can also make a *function*, whose value depends upon some input (we call this input an *argument* – we will be using the word "input" later in the book to mean something different):

OCaml

9

```
# let cube x = x * x * x;;
val cube : int -> int = <fun>
# cube 200;;
- : int = 8000000
```

We chose cube for the name of the function and x for the name of its argument. When we typed the function in, OCaml replied by telling us that its type is int → int. This means it is a function which takes an integer as its argument, and, when given that argument, evaluates to an integer. To use the function, we just write its name followed by a suitable argument. In our example, we calculated 200^3 by giving the cube function 200 as its argument.

The cube function has type int → int, we gave it an integer 200, and so the result is another integer. Thus, the type of the expression cube 200 is int – remember that the type of any expression is the type of the thing it will evaluate to, and cube 200 evaluates to 8000000, an integer. In diagram form:

If we try an argument of the wrong type, the program will be rejected:

        OCaml

```
# let cube x = x * x * x;;
val cube : int -> int = <fun>
# cube false;;
Error: This expression has type bool but an expression was expected of type
        int
```

Here is a function which determines if an integer is negative:

        OCaml

```
# let neg x = if x < 0 then true else false;;
val neg : int -> bool = <fun>
# neg (-30);;                              we add parentheses to distinguish from neg - 30
- : bool = true
```

But, of course, this is equivalent to just writing

        OCaml

```
# let neg x = x < 0;;
val neg : int -> bool = <fun>
# neg (-30);;
- : bool = true
```

because x < 0 will evaluate to the appropriate boolean value on its own – true if x < 0 and false otherwise. Here is another function, this time of type char → bool. It determines if a given character is a vowel or not:

```
            OCaml

# let isvowel c =
    c = 'a' || c = 'e' || c = 'i' || c = 'o' || c = 'u';;
val isvowel : char -> bool = <fun>
# isvowel 'x';;
- : bool = false
```

Notice that we typed the function over two lines. This can be done by pressing the Enter key in between lines. OCaml knows that we are finished when we type ;; followed by Enter as usual. Notice also that we pressed space a few times so that the second line appeared a little to the right of the first. This is known as *indentation* and does not affect the meaning of the program at all – it is just for readability.

There can be more than one argument to a function. For example, here is a function which checks if two numbers add up to ten:

```
            OCaml

# let addtoten a b =
    a + b = 10;;
val addtoten : int -> int -> bool = <fun>
# addtoten 6 4;;
- : bool = true
```

The type is **int** $\rightarrow$ **int** $\rightarrow$ **bool** because the arguments are both integers, and the result is a boolean. We use the function in the same way as before, but writing two integers this time, one for each argument the function expects.

A *recursive* function is one which uses itself. Consider calculating the factorial of a given number – the factorial of 4 (written 4! in mathematics), for example, is $4 \times 3 \times 2 \times 1$. Here is a recursive function to calculate the factorial of a positive number. Note that it uses itself in its own definition.

```
            OCaml

# let rec factorial a =
    if a = 1 then 1 else a * factorial (a - 1);;
val factorial : int -> int = <fun>
# factorial 4;;
- : int = 24
```

We used **let rec** instead of **let** to indicate a recursive function. How does the evaluation of factorial 4 proceed?

$$
\begin{array}{ll}
& \underline{\texttt{factorial 4}} \\
\implies & \texttt{4 * }\underline{\texttt{factorial 3}} \\
\implies & \texttt{4 * (3 * }\underline{\texttt{factorial 2}}\texttt{)} \\
\implies & \texttt{4 * (3 * (2 * }\underline{\texttt{factorial 1}}\texttt{))} \\
\implies & \texttt{4 * (3 * }\underline{\texttt{(2 * 1)}}\texttt{)} \\
\implies & \texttt{4 * }\underline{\texttt{(3 * 2)}} \\
\implies & \underline{\texttt{4 * 6}} \\
\implies & \texttt{24}
\end{array}
$$

For the first three steps, the **else** part of the conditional expression is chosen, because the argument a is greater than one. When the argument is equal to one, we do not use `factorial` again, but just evaluate to one. The expression built up of all the multiplications is then evaluated until a value is reached: this is the result of the whole evaluation. It is sometimes possible for a recursive function never to finish – what if we try to evaluate `factorial (-1)`?

$$
\begin{aligned}
&\underline{\text{factorial } (-1)} \\
\Longrightarrow\quad &-1 * \underline{\text{factorial } (-2)} \\
\Longrightarrow\quad &-1 * (-2 * \underline{\text{factorial } (-3)}) \\
\Longrightarrow\quad &-1 * (-2 * (-3 * \underline{\text{factorial } (-4)})) \\
&\qquad\vdots\qquad\vdots
\end{aligned}
$$

The expression keeps expanding, and the recursion keeps going. Helpfully, OCaml tells us what is going on:

```
      OCaml

# let rec factorial a =
    if a = 1 then 1 else a * factorial (a - 1);;
val factorial : int -> int = <fun>
# factorial (-1);;
Stack overflow during evaluation (looping recursion?).
```

This is an example of an error OCaml cannot find by merely looking at the program – it can only be detected during evaluation. Later in the book, we will see how to prevent people who are using our functions from making such mistakes.

One of the oldest methods for solving a problem (called *algorithms*) still in common use is Euclid's algorithm for calculating the greatest common divisor of two numbers (that is, given two positive integers a and b, finding the biggest positive integer c such that neither a/c nor b/c have a remainder). Euclid was a Greek mathematician who lived about three centuries before Christ. Euclid's algorithm is simple to write as a function with two arguments:

```
      OCaml

# let rec gcd a b =
    if b = 0 then a else gcd b (a mod b);;
val gcd : int -> int -> int = <fun>
# gcd 64000 3456;;
- : int = 128
```

Here is the evaluation:

$$
\begin{aligned}
&\underline{\text{gcd } 64000\ 3456} \\
\Longrightarrow\quad &\underline{\text{gcd } 3456\ 1792} \\
\Longrightarrow\quad &\underline{\text{gcd } 1792\ 1664} \\
\Longrightarrow\quad &\underline{\text{gcd } 1664\ 128} \\
\Longrightarrow\quad &\underline{\text{gcd } 128\ 0} \\
\Longrightarrow\quad &128
\end{aligned}
$$

Finally, here is a simple function on boolean values. In the previous chapter, we looked at the && and ||
operators which are built in to OCaml. The other important boolean operator is the not function, which
returns the boolean complement (opposite) of its argument – true if the argument is false, and vice versa.
This is also built in, but it is easy enough to define ourselves, as a function of type **bool** → **bool**.

        OCaml

```
# let not x =
    if x then false else true;;
val not : bool -> bool = <fun>
# not true;;
- : bool = false
```

Almost every program we write will involve functions such as these, and many larger ones too. In fact,
languages like OCaml are often called *functional languages*.

Questions

1. Write a function which multiplies a given number by ten. What is its type?

2. Write a function which returns `true` if both of its arguments are non-zero, and `false` otherwise. What is the type of your function?

3. Write a recursive function which, given a number n, calculates the sum $1 + 2 + 3 + \ldots + n$. What is its type?

4. Write a function `power x n` which raises x to the power n. Give its type.

5. Write a function `isconsonant` which, given a lower-case character in the range `'a'...'z'`, determines if it is a consonant.

6. What is the result of the expression **let** x = 1 **in let** x = 2 **in** x + x ?

7. Can you suggest a way of preventing the non-termination of the `factorial` function in the case of a zero or negative argument?

So Far

1 Integers `min_int` ... `-3 -2 -1 0 1 2 3` ... `max_int` of type **int**. Booleans `true` and `false` of type **bool**. Characters of type **char** like `'X'` and `'!'`.

Mathematical operators `+ - * /` `mod` which take two integers and give another.

Operators `= < <= > >= <>` which compare two values and evaluate to either `true` or `false`.

The conditional **if** *expression1* **then** *expression2* **else** *expression3*, where *expresssion1* has type **bool** and *expression2* and *expression3* have the same type as one another.

The boolean operators `&&` and `||` which allow us to build compound boolean expressions.

2 Assigning a name to the result of evaluating an expression using the **let** *name* = *expression* construct. Building compound expressions using **let** *name1* = *expression1* **in** **let** *name2* = *expression2* **in** ...

Functions, introduced by **let** *name argument1 argument2* ... = *expression*. These have type $\alpha \rightarrow \beta$, $\alpha \rightarrow \beta \rightarrow \gamma$ etc. for some types α, β, γ etc.

Recursive functions, which are introduced in the same way, but using **let rec** instead of **let**.

Note on Notation

From now on, instead of showing the actual OCaml session...

```
        OCaml

# let rec factorial a =
    if a = 1 then 1 else a * factorial (a - 1);;
val factorial : int -> int = <fun>
```

...we will usually just show the program in a box, together with its type:

```
factorial : int → int

let rec factorial a =
  if a = 1 then 1 else a * factorial (a - 1)
```

If you prefer to compose your programs in a text editing program, and copy-and-paste them into OCaml, you can do that too. Just make sure you end with ;; to let OCaml know you have finished entering the program.

Later on, when we write larger programs, we will see how to use OCaml to load our programs from external files.

Chapter 3

Case by Case

In the previous chapter, we used the conditional expression **if** ... **then** ... **else** to define functions whose results depend on their arguments. For some of them we had to nest the conditional expressions one inside another. Programs like this are not terribly easy to read, and expand quickly in size and complexity as the number of cases increases.

OCaml has a nicer way of expressing choices – *pattern matching*. For example, recall our factorial function:

```
factorial : int → int

let rec factorial a =
  if a = 1 then 1 else a * factorial (a - 1)
```

We can rewrite this using pattern matching:

```
factorial : int → int

let rec factorial a =
  match a with
    1 -> 1
  | _ -> a * factorial (a - 1)
```

We can read this as "See if a matches the pattern 1. If it does, just return 1. If not, see if it matches the pattern _. If it does, the result is a * factorial (a - 1)." The pattern _ is special – it matches anything. Remember our isvowel function from the previous chapter?

```
isvowel : char → bool

let isvowel c =
  c = 'a' || c = 'e' || c = 'i' || c = 'o' || c = 'u'
```

Here is how to write it using pattern matching:

```
isvowel : char → bool

let isvowel c =
  match c with
    'a' -> true
  | 'e' -> true
  | 'i' -> true
  | 'o' -> true
  | 'u' -> true
  | _ -> false
```

If we miss out one or more cases, OCaml will warn us:

```
                OCaml

# let isvowel c =
    match c with
      'a' -> true
    | 'e' -> true
    | 'i' -> true
    | 'o' -> true
    | 'u' -> true;;
# Warning 8: this pattern-matching is not exhaustive.
Here is an example of a value that is not matched:
'b'
val isvowel : char -> bool
```

OCaml does not reject the program, because there may be legitimate reasons to miss cases out, but for now we will make sure all our pattern matches are complete. Notice that we had to repeat true five times. This would be awkward if the expression to be calculated was more complicated. We can combine patterns like this:

```
isvowel : char → bool

let isvowel c =
  match c with
    'a' | 'e' | 'i' | 'o' | 'u' -> true
  | _ -> false
```

Finally, let us rewrite Euclid's Algorithm from the previous chapter:

```
gcd : int → int → int

let rec gcd a b =
  if b = 0 then a else gcd b (a mod b)
```

Now in pattern matching style:

```
gcd : int → int → int

let rec gcd a b =
  match b with
    0 -> a
  | _ -> gcd b (a mod b)
```

The type of a whole **match** ... **with** ... expression is determined by the types of the expressions on the right hand side of each -> arrow, all of which must be alike:

$$\underbrace{\texttt{match b with 0 -> } \overbrace{\texttt{a}}^{\text{int}} \texttt{ | \_ -> } \overbrace{\texttt{gcd b (a mod b)}}^{\text{int}}}_{\text{int}}$$

We use pattern matching whenever it is easier to read and understand than **if** ... **then** ... **else** expressions.

Questions

1. Rewrite the not function from the previous chapter in pattern matching style.

2. Use pattern matching to write a recursive function which, given a positive integer n, returns the sum of all the integers from 1 to n.

3. Use pattern matching to write a function which, given two numbers x and n, computes x^n.

4. For each of the previous three questions, comment on whether you think it is easier to read the function with or without pattern matching. How might you expect this to change if the functions were much larger?

5. What does `match 1 + 1 with 2 -> match 2 + 2 with 3 -> 4 | 4 -> 5` evaluate to?

6. There is a special pattern `x..y` to denote continuous ranges of characters, for example `'a'..'z'` will match all lowercase letters. Write functions `islower` and `isupper`, each of type **char** $\rightarrow$ **bool**, to decide on the case of a given letter.

So Far

1 Integers min_int ... -3 -2 -1 0 1 2 3 ... max_int of type **int**. Booleans true and false of type **bool**. Characters of type **char** like 'X' and '!'.

Mathematical operators + - * / mod which take two integers and give another.

Operators = < <= > >= <> which compare two values and evaluate to either true or false.

The conditional **if** *expression1* **then** *expression2* **else** *expression3*, where *expresssion1* has type **bool** and *expression2* and *expression3* have the same type as one another.

The boolean operators && and || which allow us to build compound boolean expressions.

2 Assigning a name to the result of evaluating an expression using the **let** *name* = *expression* construct. Building compound expressions using **let** *name1* = *expression1* **in** **let** *name2* = *expression2* **in** ...

Functions, introduced by **let** *name argument1 argument2* ... = *expression*. These have type $\alpha \rightarrow \beta$, $\alpha \rightarrow \beta \rightarrow \gamma$ etc. for some types α, β, γ etc.

Recursive functions, which are introduced in the same way, but using **let rec** instead of **let**.

3 Matching patterns using **match** *expression1* **with** *pattern1* | ... -> *expression2* | *pattern2* | ... -> *expression3* | ... The expressions *expression2*, *expression3* etc. must have the same type as one another, and this is the type of the whole **match ... with** expression.

Chapter 4

Making Lists

A *list* is a collection of elements. Here is a list of three integers:

```
[1; 2; 3]
```

We write a list between square brackets [and], separating the elements with semicolons. The list above has type **int list**, because it is a list of integers. All elements of the list must have the same type. The elements in the list are ordered (in other words, [1; 2; 3] and [2; 3; 1] are not the same list).

The first element is called the *head*, and the rest are collectively called the *tail*. In our example, the head is the integer 1 and the tail is the list [2; 3]. So you can see that the tail has the same type as the whole list. Here is a list with no elements (called "the empty list" or sometimes "nil"):

```
[]
```

It has neither a head nor a tail. Here is a list with just a single element:

```
[5]
```

Its head is the integer 5 and its tail is the empty list []. So every non-empty list has both a head and a tail. Lists may contain elements of any type: integers, booleans, functions, even other lists. For example, here is a list containing elements of type **bool**:

```
[false; true; false]  : bool list
```

OCaml defines two operators for lists. The :: operator (pronounced "cons") is used to add a single element to the front of an existing list:

$$
\begin{aligned}
&\texttt{false :: [true; false]} \\
\implies \quad &\texttt{[false; true; false]}
\end{aligned}
$$

The cons operation is completed in a constant amount of time, regardless of the length of the list. The @ operator (pronounced "append") is used to combine two lists together:

$$
\begin{aligned}
&\texttt{[1; 2] @ [3; 4; 5]} \\
\implies \quad &\texttt{[1; 2; 3; 4; 5]}
\end{aligned}
$$

25

This takes time proportional to the length of the list on the left hand side of the @ operator (that is, a list of length 100 will take roughly twice as long as one of length 50). We will see why soon.

Now, how do we write functions using lists? We can use pattern matching as usual, with some new types of pattern. For example, here's a function which tells us if a list is empty:

```
isnil : α list → bool

let isnil l =
  match l with
    [] -> true                                    the list is empty
  | _ -> false                           it has at least one element
```

The argument has type α **list** (which OCaml prints on the screen as 'a list) because this function does not inspect the individual elements of the list, it just checks if the list is empty. And so, this function can operate over any type of list. The greek letters α, β, γ etc. stand for any type. If two types are represented by the same greek letter they must have the same type. If they are not, they may have the same type, but do not have to. Functions like this are known as *polymorphic*. We can also use :: in our patterns, this time using it to deconstruct rather than construct the list:

```
length : α list → int

let rec length l =
  match l with
    [] -> 0                      the list has zero elements (the "base case")
  | h::t -> 1 + length t                       h is the head, t the tail
```

Here is how the evaluation proceeds:

$$
\begin{aligned}
&\texttt{length [5; 5; 5]}\\
\Longrightarrow\quad &\texttt{1 + length [5; 5]}\\
\Longrightarrow\quad &\texttt{1 + (1 + length [5])}\\
\Longrightarrow\quad &\texttt{1 + (1 + (1 + length []))} \qquad \textit{base case}\\
\Longrightarrow\quad &\texttt{1 + (1 + (1 + 0))}\\
\overset{*}{\Longrightarrow}\quad &\texttt{3} \qquad (\overset{*}{\Longrightarrow} \textit{ means we are not showing all the steps})
\end{aligned}
$$

This works by recursion over the list, then addition of all the resultant 1s. It takes time proportional to the length of the list. Can you see why? It also takes space proportional to the length of the list, because of the intermediate expression 1 + (1 + (1 + ... which is built up before any of the + operations are evaluated – this expression must be stored somewhere whilst it is being processed. Since h is not used in the expression 1 + length t, this function is also polymorphic. Indeed we can replace h in the pattern with _ since there is no use giving a name to something we are not going to refer to:

```
length : α list → int

let rec length l =
  match l with
    [] -> 0                       the list has zero elements
  | _::t -> 1 + length t          _ is the head, t the tail
```

A very similar function can be used to add a list of integers:

```
sum : int list → int

let rec sum l =
  match l with
    [] -> 0                          the sum of no elements is zero
  | h::t -> h + sum t       otherwise, add the head to the sum of the tail
```

However, since we are actually using the individual list elements (by adding them up), this function is not polymorphic – it operates over lists of type **int list** only. If we accidentally miss out a case, OCaml will alert us, and give an example pattern which is not matched:

```
        OCaml

# let rec sum l =
match l with =
      h::t -> h + sum t;;
Warning 8: this pattern-matching is not exhaustive.
Here is an example of a value that is not matched:
[]
val sum : int list -> int = <fun>
```

There is a way to deal with the excessive space usage from the building up of a large intermediate expression 1 + 1 + 1 + . . . in our length function, at the cost of readability. We can "accumulate" the 1s as we go along in an extra argument. At each recursive step, the accumulating argument is increased by one. When we have finished, the total is returned:

```
length_inner : α list → int → int
length : α list → int

let rec length_inner l n =
  match l with
    [] -> n                            list is empty, return the accumulator
  | h::t -> length_inner t (n + 1)   add one to the accumulator, and carry on

let length l = length_inner l 0           give an initial accumulator of zero
```

We wrapped it up in another function to make sure we do not call it with a bad initial value for the accumulating argument. Here is an example evaluation:

$$
\begin{array}{ll}
& \texttt{length [5; 5; 5]} \\
\implies & \texttt{length\_inner [5; 5; 5] 0} \\
\implies & \texttt{length\_inner [5; 5] 1} \\
\implies & \texttt{length\_inner [5] 2} \\
\implies & \texttt{length\_inner [] 3} \qquad \textit{base case} \\
\implies & \texttt{3}
\end{array}
$$

Now, the space taken by the calculation does not relate in any way to the length of the list argument. Recursive functions which do not build up a growing intermediate expression are known as *tail recursive*. Functions can, of course, return lists too. Here is a function to return the list consisting of the first, third, fifth and so on elements in a list:

```
odd_elements : α list → α list

let rec odd_elements l =
  match l with
    [] -> []                              the list has zero elements
  | [a] -> [a]                            the list has one element
  | a::_::t -> a :: odd_elements t        the list has more than one element
```

Consider the evaluation of `odd_elements [2; 4; 2; 4; 2]`:

$$
\begin{array}{ll}
& \texttt{odd\_elements [2; 4; 2; 4; 2]} \\
\implies & \texttt{2 :: odd\_elements [2; 4; 2]} \\
\implies & \texttt{2 :: 2 :: odd\_elements [2]} \\
\implies & \texttt{2 :: 2 :: [2]} \\
\overset{*}{\implies} & \texttt{[2; 2; 2]}
\end{array}
$$

You might notice that the first two cases in the pattern match return exactly their argument. By reversing the order, we can reduce this function to just two cases:

```
odd_elements : α list → α list

let rec odd_elements l =
  match l with
    a::_::t -> a :: odd_elements t        there is something to skip over
  | _ -> l                                there is nothing to skip over
```

We have seen how to use the @ (append) operator to concatenate two lists:

$$
\begin{array}{ll}
& \texttt{[1; 2] @ [3; 4; 5]} \\
\implies & \texttt{[1; 2; 3; 4; 5]}
\end{array}
$$

How might we implement list append ourselves, if it was not provided? Consider a function append a b. If the list a is the empty list, the answer is simply b. But what if a is not empty? Then it has a head h and a tail t. So we can start our result list with the head, and the rest of the result is just append t b.

```
append : α list → α list → α list

let rec append a b =
  match a with
    [] -> b
  | h::t -> h :: append t b
```

Consider the evaluation of append [1; 2; 3] [4; 5; 6]:

$$
\begin{aligned}
&\qquad\text{append } [1;\ 2;\ 3]\ [4;\ 5;\ 6] \\
\Longrightarrow\quad &1\ ::\ \text{append } [2;\ 3]\ [4;\ 5;\ 6] \\
\Longrightarrow\quad &1\ ::\ 2\ ::\ \text{append } [3]\ [4;\ 5;\ 6] \\
\Longrightarrow\quad &1\ ::\ 2\ ::\ 3\ ::\ \text{append } []\ [4;\ 5;\ 6] \\
\Longrightarrow\quad &1\ ::\ 2\ ::\ 3\ ::\ [4;\ 5;\ 6] \\
\overset{*}{\Longrightarrow}\quad &[1;\ 2;\ 3;\ 4;\ 5;\ 6]
\end{aligned}
$$

This takes time proportional to the length of the first list – the second list need not be processed at all. What about reversing a list? For example, we want rev [1; 2; 3; 4] to evaluate to [4; 3; 2; 1]. One simple way is to reverse the tail of the list, and append the list just containing the head to the end of it:

```
rev : α list → α list

let rec rev l =
  match l with
    [] -> []
  | h::t -> rev t @ [h]
```

Here's how the evaluation proceeds:

$$
\begin{aligned}
&\qquad\text{rev } [1;\ 2;\ 3;\ 4] \\
\Longrightarrow\quad &\text{rev } [2;\ 3;\ 4]\ @\ [1] \\
\Longrightarrow\quad &\text{rev } [3;\ 4]\ @\ [2]\ @\ [1] \\
\Longrightarrow\quad &\text{rev } [4]\ @\ [3]\ @\ [2]\ @\ [1] \\
\Longrightarrow\quad &\text{rev } []\ @\ [4]\ @\ [3]\ @\ [2]\ @\ [1] \\
\Longrightarrow\quad &[]\ @\ [4]\ @\ [3]\ @\ [2]\ @\ [1] \\
\overset{*}{\Longrightarrow}\quad &[4;\ 3;\ 2;\ 1]
\end{aligned}
$$

This is a simple definition, but not very efficient – can you see why?

Two more useful functions for processing lists are take and drop which, given a number and a list, either take or drop that many elements from the list:

```
take : int → α list → α list
drop : int → α list → α list

let rec take n l =
  if n = 0 then [] else
    match l with
      h::t -> h :: take (n - 1) t

let rec drop n l =
  if n = 0 then l else
    match l with
      h::t -> drop (n - 1) t
```

For example, here's the evaluation for take 2 [2; 4; 6; 8; 10]:

$$\begin{array}{rl} & \underline{\text{take 2 [2; 4; 6; 8; 10]}} \\ \Longrightarrow & 2 :: \underline{\text{take 1 [4; 6; 8; 10]}} \\ \Longrightarrow & 2 :: 4 :: \underline{\text{take 0 [6; 8; 10]}} \\ \Longrightarrow & \underline{2 :: 4 :: []} \\ \overset{*}{\Longrightarrow} & [2; 4] \end{array}$$

And for drop 2 [2; 4; 6; 8; 10]:

$$\begin{array}{rl} & \underline{\text{drop 2 [2; 4; 6; 8; 10]}} \\ & \underline{\text{drop 1 [4; 6; 8; 10]}} \\ \Longrightarrow & \underline{\text{drop 0 [6; 8; 10]}} \\ \Longrightarrow & [6; 8; 10] \end{array}$$

Note that these functions contain incomplete pattern matches – OCaml tells us so when we type them in. The function fails if the arguments are not sensible – that is, when we are asked to take or drop more elements than are in the argument list. Later on, we will see how to deal with that problem. Note also that for any sensible value of n, including zero, take n l and drop n l split the list into two parts with no gap. So drop and take often appear in pairs.

Lists can contain anything, so long as all elements are of the same type. So, of course, a list can contain lists. Here's a list of lists of integers:

[[1]; [2; 3]; [4; 5; 6]] : (int list) list   *We can also just write **int list list***

Each element of this list is of type **int list**. Within values of this type, it is important to distinguish the list of lists containing no elements

[] : α list list

from the list of lists containing one element which is the empty list

[[]] : α list list

Questions

1. Write a function `evens` which does the opposite to `odds`, returning the even numbered elements in a list. For example, `evens [2; 4; 2; 4; 2]` should return `[4; 4]`. What is the type of your function?

2. Write a function `count_true` which counts the number of `true` elements in a list. For example, `count_true [true; false; true]` should return 2. What is the type of your function? Can you write a tail recursive version?

3. Write a function which, given a list, builds a palindrome from it. A palindrome is a list which equals its own reverse. You can assume the existence of `rev` and `@`. Write another function which determines if a list is a palindrome.

4. Write a function `drop_last` which returns all but the last element of a list. If the list is empty, it should return the empty list. So, for example, `drop_last [1; 2; 4; 8]` should return `[1; 2; 4]`. What about a tail recursive version?

5. Write a function `member` of type $\alpha \rightarrow \alpha$ **list** $\rightarrow$ **bool** which returns `true` if an element exists in a list, or `false` if not. For example, `member 2 [1; 2; 3]` should evaluate to `true`, but `member 3 [1; 2]` should evaluate to `false`.

6. Use your `member` function to write a function `make_set` which, given a list, returns a list which contains all the elements of the original list, but has no duplicate elements. For example, `make_set [1; 2; 3; 3; 1]` might return `[2; 3; 1]`. What is the type of your function?

7. Can you explain why the `rev` function we defined is inefficient? How does the time it takes to run relate to the size of its argument? Can you write a more efficient version using an accumulating argument? What is its efficiency in terms of time taken and space used?

So Far

1 Integers `min_int` ... `-3 -2 -1 0 1 2 3` ... `max_int` of type **int**. Booleans `true` and `false` of type **bool**. Characters of type **char** like `'X'` and `'!'`.

Mathematical operators `+ - * / mod` which take two integers and give another.

Operators `= < <= > >= <>` which compare two values and evaluate to either `true` or `false`.

The conditional **if** *expression1* **then** *expression2* **else** *expression3*, where *expresssion1* has type **bool** and *expression2* and *expression3* have the same type as one another.

The boolean operators `&&` and `||` which allow us to build compound boolean expressions.

2 Assigning a name to the result of evaluating an expression using the **let** *name* = *expression* construct. Building compound expressions using **let** *name1* = *expression1* **in** **let** *name2* = *expression2* **in** ...

Functions, introduced by **let** *name argument1 argument2* ... = *expression*. These have type $\alpha \to \beta$, $\alpha \to \beta \to \gamma$ etc. for some types α, β, γ etc.

Recursive functions, which are introduced in the same way, but using **let rec** instead of **let**.

3 Matching patterns using **match** *expression1* **with** *pattern1* | ... -> *expression2* | *pattern2* | ... -> *expression3* | ... The expressions *expression2*, *expression3* etc. must have the same type as one another, and this is the type of the whole **match** ... **with** expression.

4 Lists, which are ordered collections of zero or more elements of like type. They are written between square brackets, with elements separated by semicolons e.g. `[1; 2; 3; 4; 5]`. If a list is non-empty, it has a head, which is its first element, and a tail, which is the list composed of the rest of the elements.

The `::` "cons" operator, which adds an element to the front of a list. The `@` "append" operator, which concatenates two lists together.

Lists and the `::` "cons" symbol may be used for pattern matching to distinguish lists of length zero, one, etc. and with particular contents.

Two Different Ways of Thinking

Look again at our list appending function:

```
append : α list → α list → α list

let rec append a b =
  match a with
    [] -> b
  | h::t -> h :: append t b
```

There are two ways to think about this computation. One way is to imagine the actions the computer might take to calculate the result:

Look at the first list. If it is empty, return the second list. Otherwise, pull apart the first list, looking at its head and tail. Make a recursive call to append the tail to the second list, and then cons the head onto the result. Return this.

Alternatively, we can consider each match case to be an independent statement of truth, thinking the same way about the whole function:

The empty list appended to another list is that list. Otherwise, the first list is non-empty, so it has a head and a tail. Call them h and t. Clearly append (h :: t) b is equal to h :: append t b. Since this reduces the problem size, progress is made.

It is very useful to be able to think in these two ways about functions you write, and to be able to swap between them in the mind with ease.

Chapter 5

Sorting Things

Lists often need to be in sorted order. How might we write a function to sort a list of integers? Well, a list with zero elements is already sorted. If we do not have an empty list, we must have a head and a tail. What can we do with those? Well, we can sort the tail by a recursive call to our `sort` function. So, now we have the head, and an already sorted list. Now, we just need to write a function to insert the head in an already sorted list. We have reduced the problem to an easier one.

```
let rec sort l =
  match l with
    [] -> []                         an empty list is already sorted
  | h::t -> insert h (sort t)        insert the head into the sorted tail
```

Now we just need to write the `insert` function. This takes an element and an already-sorted list, and returns the list with the element inserted in the right place:

```
let rec insert x l =
  match l with
    [] -> [x]                        the simple case – just put x in
  | h::t ->                          otherwise we have a head and a tail
      if x <= h                      if we are at an appropriate point
        then x :: h :: t             just put x here
        else h :: insert x t         otherwise, keep h and carry on
```

Consider the evaluation of `insert 3 [1; 1; 2; 3; 5; 9]`:

$$
\begin{aligned}
&\underline{\text{insert 3 [1; 1; 2; 3; 5; 9]}}\\
\Longrightarrow\quad &1 :: \underline{\text{insert 3 [1; 2; 3; 5; 9]}}\\
\Longrightarrow\quad &1 :: 1 :: \underline{\text{insert 3 [2; 3; 5; 9]}}\\
\Longrightarrow\quad &1 :: 1 :: 2 :: \underline{\text{insert 3 [3; 5; 9]}}\\
\Longrightarrow\quad &\underline{1 :: 1 :: 2 :: 3 :: 3 :: [5; 9]}\\
\overset{*}{\Longrightarrow}\quad &[1; 1; 2; 3; 3; 5; 9]
\end{aligned}
$$

37

Here is the whole evaluation of sort [53; 9; 2; 6; 19]. We have missed out the detail of each insert operation.

sort [53; 9; 2; 6; 19]

$\overset{*}{\Longrightarrow}$ insert 53 (sort [9; 2; 6; 19])

$\overset{*}{\Longrightarrow}$ insert 53 (insert 9 (sort [2; 6; 19]))

$\overset{*}{\Longrightarrow}$ insert 53 (insert 9 (insert 2 (sort [6; 19])))

$\overset{*}{\Longrightarrow}$ insert 53 (insert 9 (insert 2 (insert 6 (sort [19]))))

$\overset{*}{\Longrightarrow}$ insert 53 (insert 9 (insert 2 (insert 6 (insert 19 (sort [])))))

$\overset{*}{\Longrightarrow}$ insert 53 (insert 9 (insert 2 (insert 6 (insert 19 []))))

$\overset{*}{\Longrightarrow}$ insert 53 (insert 9 (insert 2 (insert 6 [19])))

$\overset{*}{\Longrightarrow}$ insert 53 (insert 9 (insert 2 [6; 19]))

$\overset{*}{\Longrightarrow}$ insert 53 (insert 9 [2; 6; 19])

$\overset{*}{\Longrightarrow}$ insert 53 [2; 6; 9; 19]

$\overset{*}{\Longrightarrow}$ [2; 6; 9; 19; 53]

Here's the full program, known as *insertion sort*:

```
insert : α → α list → α list
sort : α list → α list

let rec insert x l =
  match l with
    [] -> [x]
  | h::t ->
      if x <= h
        then x :: h :: t
        else h :: insert x t

let rec sort l =
  match l with
    [] -> []
  | h::t -> insert h (sort t)
```

Notice that the type α list → α list rather than **int** list → **int** list. This is because OCaml's comparison functions like <= (used inside insert) work for types other than **int**. For example, OCaml knows how to compare characters in alphabetical order:

sort ['p'; 'i'; 'm'; 'c'; 's'; 'h']

$\overset{*}{\Longrightarrow}$ ['c'; 'h'; 'i'; 'm'; 'p'; 's']

How long does our sorting function take to run if the list to be sorted has n elements? Under the assumption that our argument list is arbitrarily ordered rather than sorted, each insert operation takes time proportional to n (the element might need to be inserted anywhere). We must run the insert function as many times as there are elements so, adding these all up, the sort function takes time proportional to n^2. You might argue that the first insert operations only have to work with a very small list, and that this fact should make the time less that n^2. Can you see why that is not true? What happens if the list is sorted already?

A more efficient algorithm can be found by considering a basic operation a little more complex than insert, but which still operates in time proportional to the length of the argument list. Such a function is merge, which takes two already sorted lists, and returns a single sorted list:

```
merge : α list → α list → α list

let rec merge x y =
  match x, y with            we can match on more than one thing using commas
    [], l -> l                          if the first is empty, just return the second
  | l, [] -> l                                                    and vice-versa
  | hx::tx, hy::ty ->
      if hx < hy
        then hx :: merge tx (hy :: ty)     put hx first because it is smaller
        else hy :: merge (hx :: tx) ty                  otherwise put hy first
```

When x and y are both the empty list, the first case is picked because l matches the empty list. Here is how merge proceeds:

$$
\begin{array}{ll}
& \underline{\text{merge [9; 53] [2; 6; 19]}} \\
\Longrightarrow & 2 :: (\underline{\text{merge [9; 53] [6; 19]}}) \\
\Longrightarrow & 2 :: 6 :: (\underline{\text{merge [9; 53] [19]}}) \\
\Longrightarrow & 2 :: 6 :: 9 :: (\underline{\text{merge [53] [19]}}) \\
\Longrightarrow & 2 :: 6 :: 9 :: 19 :: (\underline{\text{merge [53] []}}) \\
\Longrightarrow & 2 :: 6 :: 9 :: 19 :: \underline{\text{[53]}} \\
\overset{*}{\Longrightarrow} & [2; 6; 9; 19; 53]
\end{array}
$$

So merge can take two sorted lists, and produce a longer, sorted list, containing all the elements from both lists. So, how can we use this to sort a list from scratch? Well, we can use length, take, and drop from the previous chapter to split the list into two halves. Now, we must use a recursive call to sort each half, and then we can merge them. This is known as *merge sort*.

```
msort : α list → α list

let rec msort l =
  match l with
    [] -> []                                we are done if the list is empty
  | [x] -> [x]                              also if it has only one element
  | _ ->
      let left = take (length l / 2) l in          get the left hand half
        let right = drop (length l / 2) l in      and the right hand half
          merge (msort left) (msort right)       sort sublists and merge
```

The case for the single element is required because, if we split it into two halves, of length one and zero, the recursion would not end – we would not have reduced the size of the problem.

How does msort work? Consider the evaluation of msort on the list [53; 9; 2; 6; 19]. We will skip the evaluation of the merge, drop, take, and length functions, concentrating just on msort:

```
        msort [53; 9; 2; 6; 19]
  *
  ⟹    merge (msort [53; 9]) (msort [2; 6; 19])
  *
  ⟹    merge (merge (msort [53]) (msort [9])) (msort [2; 6; 19])
  *
  ⟹    merge (merge [53] (msort [9])) (msort [2; 6; 19])
  *
  ⟹    merge (merge [53] [9]) (msort [2; 6; 19])
  *
  ⟹    merge [9; 53] (msort [2; 6; 19])
  *
  ⟹    merge [9; 53] (merge (msort [2]) (msort [6; 19])
  *
  ⟹    merge [9; 53] (merge [2] (msort [6; 19]))
  *
  ⟹    merge [9; 53] (merge [2] (merge (msort [6]) (msort [19])))
  *
  ⟹    merge [9; 53] (merge [2] (merge [6] (msort [19])))
  *
  ⟹    merge [9; 53] (merge [2] (merge [6] [19]))
  *
  ⟹    merge [9; 53] (merge [2] [6; 19])
  *
  ⟹    merge [9; 53] [2; 6; 19]
  *
  ⟹    [2; 6; 9; 19; 53]
```

From now on we will not be showing these full evaluations all the time – but when you are unsure of how or why a function works, you can always write them out on paper yourself.

How long does it take?

How long does merge sort take to run? We can visualize it with the following diagram, in which we have chosen a list of length eight (a power of two) for convenience.

```
[6; 4; 5; 7; 2; 5; 3; 4]
[6; 4; 5; 7][2; 5; 3; 4]
[6; 4][5; 7][2; 5][3; 4]
[6][4][5][7][2][5][3][4]
[4; 6][5; 7][2; 5][3; 4]
[4; 5; 6; 7][2; 3; 4; 5]
[2; 3; 4; 4; 5; 5; 6; 7]
```

In the top half of the diagram, the lists are being taken apart using take and drop, until they are small enough to already be sorted. In the bottom half, they are being merged back together.

How long does each row take? For the top half: to split a list into two halves takes time proportional to the length of the list. On the first line, we do this once on a list of length eight. On the second line, we do it twice on lists of length four, and so on. So each line takes the same time overall. For the bottom half, we have another function which takes time proportional to the length of its argument – merge – so each line in the bottom half takes time proportional to the length too.

So, how many lines do we have? Well, in the top half we have roughly $\log_2 n$, and the same for the bottom half. So, the total work done is $2 \times \log_2 n \times n$, which is proportional to $n \log_2 n$.

Questions

1. In `msort`, we calculate the value of the expression `length l / 2` twice. Modify `msort` to remove this inefficiency.

2. We know that `take` and `drop` can fail if called with incorrect arguments. Show that this is never the case in `msort`.

3. Write a version of insertion sort which sorts the argument list into reverse order.

4. Write a function to detect if a list is already in sorted order.

5. We mentioned that the comparison functions like `<` work for many OCaml types. Can you determine, by experimentation, how they work for lists? For example, what is the result of `[1; 2] < [2; 3]`? What happens when we sort the following list of type **char list list**? Why?

    ```
    [['o'; 'n'; 'e']; ['t'; 'w'; 'o']; ['t'; 'h'; 'r'; 'e'; 'e']]
    ```

6. Combine the `sort` and `insert` functions into a single `sort` function.

So Far

1 Integers min_int ... -3 -2 -1 0 1 2 3 ... max_int of type **int**. Booleans true and false of type **bool**. Characters of type **char** like 'X' and '!'.

Mathematical operators + - * / mod which take two integers and give another.

Operators = < <= > >= <> which compare two values and evaluate to either true or false.

The conditional **if** *expression1* **then** *expression2* **else** *expression3*, where *expresssion1* has type **bool** and *expression2* and *expression3* have the same type as one another.

The boolean operators && and || which allow us to build compound boolean expressions.

2 Assigning a name to the result of evaluating an expression using the **let** *name* = *expression* construct. Building compound expressions using **let** *name1* = *expression1* **in** **let** *name2* = *expression2* **in** ...

Functions, introduced by **let** *name argument1 argument2* ... = *expression*. These have type $\alpha \rightarrow \beta$, $\alpha \rightarrow \beta \rightarrow \gamma$ etc. for some types α, β, γ etc.

Recursive functions, which are introduced in the same way, but using **let rec** instead of **let**.

3 Matching patterns using **match** *expression1* **with** *pattern1* | ... -> *expression2* | *pattern2* | ... -> *expression3* | ... The expressions *expression2*, *expression3* etc. must have the same type as one another, and this is the type of the whole **match ... with** expression.

4 Lists, which are ordered collections of zero or more elements of like type. They are written between square brackets, with elements separated by semicolons e.g. [1; 2; 3; 4; 5]. If a list is non-empty, it has a head, which is its first element, and a tail, which is the list composed of the rest of the elements.

The :: "cons" operator, which adds an element to the front of a list. The @ "append" operator, which concatenates two lists together.

Lists and the :: "cons" symbol may be used for pattern matching to distinguish lists of length zero, one, etc. and with particular contents.

5 Matching two or more things at once, using commas to separate as in **match** a, b **with** 0, 0 -> *expression1* | x, y -> *expression2* | ...

Loading a Program from a File

Now that we are building larger functions, we might like to store them between sessions, rather than typing them in every time. For example, compose a file like this in a text editor:

```
let rec length l =
  match l with
    [] -> 0
  | h::t -> 1 + length t

let rec append a b =
  match a with
    [] -> b
  | h::t -> h :: append t b
```

Save the file in same directory (folder) as you enter OCaml from, under the name lists.ml. We can then tell OCaml to use the contents of that file like this:

```
          OCaml

# #use "lists.ml";;
val length : 'a list -> int = <fun>
val append : 'a list -> 'a list -> 'a list = <fun>
```

It is exactly the same as typing it in manually – the functions length and append will now be available for use. Errors and warnings will be reported as usual. Note that the #use command is not part of the OCaml language for expressions – it is just a command we are giving to OCaml.

Chapter 6

Functions upon Functions upon Functions

Often we need to apply a function to every element of a list. For example, doubling each of the numbers in a list of integers. We could do this with a simple recursive function, working over each element of a list:

```
double : int list → int list

let rec double l =
  match l with
    [] -> []                              no element to process
  | h::t -> (h * 2) :: double t    process the element, and the rest
```

For example,

$$
\begin{aligned}
&\text{double [1; 2; 4]} \\
\implies\ &\text{2 :: double [2; 4]} \\
\implies\ &\text{2 :: 4 :: double [4]} \\
\implies\ &\text{2 :: 4 :: 8 :: double []} \\
\implies\ &\text{2 :: 4 :: 8 :: []} \\
\overset{*}{\implies}\ &\text{[2; 4; 8]}
\end{aligned}
$$

The result list does not need to have the same type as the argument list. We can write a function which, given a list of integers, returns the list containing a boolean for each: true if the number is even, false if it is odd.

```
evens : int list → bool list

let rec evens l =
  match l with
    [] -> []                                    no element to process
  | h::t -> (h mod 2 = 0) :: evens t    process the element, and the rest
```

47

For example,

$$
\begin{array}{rl}
& \underline{\text{evens [1; 2; 4]}} \\
\Longrightarrow & \text{false :: } \underline{\text{evens [2; 4]}} \\
\Longrightarrow & \text{false :: true :: } \underline{\text{evens [4]}} \\
\Longrightarrow & \text{false :: true :: true :: } \underline{\text{evens []}} \\
\Longrightarrow & \underline{\text{false :: true :: true :: []}} \\
\stackrel{*}{\Longrightarrow} & \text{[false; true; true]}
\end{array}
$$

It would be tedious to write a similar function each time we wanted to apply a different operation to every element of a list – can we build one which works for any operation? We will add a function as an argument too:

```
map : (α → β) → α list → β list

let rec map f l =
  match l with
    [] -> []                          no element to process
  | h::t -> f h :: map f t      process the element, and the rest
```

The map function takes two arguments: a function which processes a single element, and a list. It returns a new list. We will discuss the type in a moment. For example, if we have a function halve:

```
halve : int → int

let halve x = x / 2
```

We can use map like this:

$$
\begin{array}{rl}
& \underline{\text{map halve [10; 20; 30]}} \\
\Longrightarrow & \text{5 :: } \underline{\text{map halve [20; 30]}} \\
\Longrightarrow & \text{5 :: 10 :: } \underline{\text{map halve [30]}} \\
\Longrightarrow & \text{5 :: 10 :: 15 :: } \underline{\text{map halve []}} \\
\Longrightarrow & \underline{\text{5 :: 10 :: 15 :: []}} \\
\stackrel{*}{\Longrightarrow} & \text{[5; 10; 15]}
\end{array}
$$

Now, let us look at that type: $(\alpha \to \beta) \to \alpha$ **list** $\to \beta$ **list**. We can annotate the individual parts:

$$
\underbrace{(\alpha \to \beta) \to}_{\text{function f}} \quad \underbrace{\alpha \ \textbf{list}}_{\text{argument list}} \quad \to \underbrace{\beta \ \textbf{list}}_{\text{result list}}
$$

We have to put the function f in parentheses, otherwise it would look like map had four arguments. It can have any type $\alpha \to \beta$. That is to say, it can have any argument and result types, and they do not have to be the same as each other – though they may be. The argument has type α **list** because each of its elements must be an appropriate argument for f. In the same way, the result list has type β **list** because each of its elements is a result from f (in our halve example, α and β were both **int**). We can rewrite our evens function to use map:

```
is_even : int → bool
evens : int list → bool list

let is_even x =
  x mod 2 = 0

let evens l =
  map is_even l
```

In this use of map, α was **int**, β was **bool**. We can make evens still shorter: when we are just using a function once, we can define it directly, without naming it:

```
evens : int list → bool list

let evens l =
  map (fun x -> x mod 2 = 0) l
```

This is called an *anonymous function*. It is defined using **fun**, a named argument, the -> arrow and the function definition (body) itself. For example, we can write our halving function like this:

```
fun x -> x / 2
```

and, thus, write:

$$\xrightarrow{\;*\;} \quad \begin{array}{l} \texttt{map (fun x -> x / 2) [10; 20; 30]} \\ \texttt{[5; 10; 15]} \end{array}$$

We use anonymous functions when a function is only used in one place and is relatively short, to avoid defining it separately.

In the preceding chapter we wrote a sorting function and, in one of the questions, you were asked to change the function to use a different comparison operator so that the function would sort elements into reverse order. Now, we know how to write a version of the msort function which uses any comparison function we give it. A comparison function would have type $\alpha \rightarrow \alpha \rightarrow$ **bool**. That is, it takes two elements of the same type, and returns true if the first is "greater" than the second, for some definition of "greater" – or false otherwise.

So, let us alter our merge and msort functions to take an extra argument – the comparison function. The result is shown in Figure 6.1. Now, if we make our own comparison operator:

```
greater : α → α → bool

let greater a b =
  a >= b
```

```
merge : (α → α → bool) → α list → α list → α list
msort : (α → α → bool) → α list → α list

let rec merge cmp x y =
  match x, y with
    [], l -> l
  | l, [] -> l
  | hx::tx, hy::ty ->
      if cmp hx hy                          use our comparison function
        then hx :: merge cmp tx (hy :: ty)  put hx first – it is "smaller"
        else hy :: merge cmp (hx :: tx) ty  otherwise put hy first

let rec msort cmp l =
  match l with
    [] -> []
  | [x] -> [x]
  | _ ->
      let left = take (length l / 2) l in
        let right = drop (length l / 2) l in
          merge cmp (msort cmp left) (msort cmp right)
```

Figure 6.1: Adding an extra argument to merge sort

we can use it with our new version of the msort function:

$$\text{msort greater [5; 4; 6; 2; 1]}$$
$$\overset{*}{\Longrightarrow} \quad \text{[6; 5; 4; 2; 1]}$$

In fact, we can ask OCaml to make such a function from an operator such as <= or + just by enclosing it in parentheses and spaces:

```
        OCaml

# ( <= )
- : 'a -> 'a -> bool = <fun>
# ( <= ) 4 5
- : bool = true
```

So, for example:

$$\text{msort (<=) [5; 4; 6; 2; 1]}$$
$$\overset{*}{\Longrightarrow} \quad \text{[1; 2; 4; 5; 6]}$$

and

$$\text{msort (>=) [5; 4; 6; 2; 1]}$$
$$\overset{*}{\Longrightarrow} \quad \text{[6; 5; 4; 2; 1]}$$

The techniques we have seen in this chapter are forms of *program reuse*, which is fundamental to writing manageable large programs.

Questions

1. Write a simple recursive function `calm` to replace exclamation marks in a **char list** with periods. For example `calm ['H'; 'e'; 'l'; 'p'; '!'; ' '; 'F'; 'i'; 'r'; 'e'; '!']` should evaluate to `calm ['H'; 'e'; 'l'; 'p'; '.'; ' '; 'F'; 'i'; 'r'; 'e'; '.']`. Now rewrite your function to use `map` instead of recursion. What are the types of your functions?

2. Write a function `clip` which, given an integer, clips it to the range 1 . . . 10 so that integers bigger than 10 round down to 10, and those smaller than 1 round up to 1. Write another function `cliplist` which uses this first function together with `map` to apply this clipping to a whole list of integers.

3. Express your function `cliplist` again, this time using an anonymous function instead of `clip`.

4. Write a function `apply` which, given another function, a number of times to apply it, and an initial argument for the function, will return the cumulative effect of repeatedly applying the function. For instance, `apply f 6 4` should return `f (f (f (f (f (f 4))))))`. What is the type of your function?

5. Modify the insertion sort function from the preceding chapter to take a comparison function, in the same way that we modified merge sort in this chapter. What is its type?

6. Write a function `filter` which takes a function of type $\alpha \rightarrow$ **bool** and an α **list** and returns a list of just those elements of the argument list for which the given function returns `true`.

7. Write the function `for_all` which, given a function of type $\alpha \rightarrow$ **bool** and an argument list of type α **list** evaluates to `true` if and only if the function returns `true` for every element of the list. Give examples of its use.

8. Write a function `mapl` which maps a function of type $\alpha \rightarrow \beta$ over a list of type α **list list** to produce a list of type β **list list**.

So Far

1 Integers `min_int ... -3 -2 -1 0 1 2 3 ... max_int` of type **int**. Booleans `true` and `false` of type **bool**. Characters of type **char** like `'X'` and `'!'`.

Mathematical operators `+ - * / mod` which take two integers and give another.

Operators `= < <= > >= <>` which compare two values and evaluate to either `true` or `false`.

The conditional **if** *expression1* **then** *expression2* **else** *expression3*, where *expression1* has type **bool** and *expression2* and *expression3* have the same type as one another.

The boolean operators `&&` and `||` which allow us to build compound boolean expressions.

2 Assigning a name to the result of evaluating an expression using the **let** *name = expression* construct. Building compound expressions using **let** *name1 = expression1* **in** **let** *name2 = expression2* **in** ...

Functions, introduced by **let** *name argument1 argument2* ... = *expression*. These have type $\alpha \rightarrow \beta$, $\alpha \rightarrow \beta \rightarrow \gamma$ etc. for some types α, β, γ etc.

Recursive functions, which are introduced in the same way, but using **let rec** instead of **let**.

3 Matching patterns using **match** *expression1* **with** *pattern1* | ... -> *expression2* | *pattern2* | ... -> *expression3* | ... The expressions *expression2*, *expression3* etc. must have the same type as one another, and this is the type of the whole **match ... with** expression.

4 Lists, which are ordered collections of zero or more elements of like type. They are written between square brackets, with elements separated by semicolons e.g. `[1; 2; 3; 4; 5]`. If a list is non-empty, it has a head, which is its first element, and a tail, which is the list composed of the rest of the elements.

The `::` "cons" operator, which adds an element to the front of a list. The `@` "append" operator, which concatenates two lists together.

Lists and the `::` "cons" symbol may be used for pattern matching to distinguish lists of length zero, one, etc. and with particular contents.

5 Matching two or more things at once, using commas to separate as in **match** `a, b` **with** `0, 0` -> *expression1* | `x, y` -> *expression2* | ...

6 Anonymous functions **fun** *name* -> *expression*. Making operators into functions as in `( < )` and `( + )`.

Chapter 7

When Things Go Wrong

Some of the functions we have written so far have had a single, correct answer for each possible argument. For example, there's no number we cannot halve. However, when we use more complicated types such as lists, there are plenty of functions which do not always have an answer – a list might not have a head or a tail, for example. Our take and drop functions were unsatisfactory in case of invalid arguments. For example, take 3 ['a'] would simply return []. This is bad practice – we are hiding errors rather than confronting them.

OCaml has a mechanism for reporting such *run-time* errors (these are quite different from the type errors OCaml reports when it refuses to accept a program at all). This mechanism is *exceptions*.

There are some built-in exceptions in OCaml. For example Division_by_zero, which is *raised* when a program tries to divide a number by zero:

        OCaml

```
# 10 / 0;;
Exception: Division_by_zero.
```

In order to signal bad arguments in functions like take and drop, we can rewrite them using the built-in exception Invalid_argument, which also carries a message written between double quotation marks. Typically we use this to record the name of the function which failed. Figure 7.1 shows take and drop rewritten to use the Invalid_argument exception using **raise**. Note that these functions deal with two problems of our previous versions: a negative argument, and being asked to take or drop more than the number of elements in the list.

We can define our own exceptions, using **exception**. They can carry information along with them, of a type we choose:

        OCaml

```
# exception Problem;;
exception Problem
# exception NotPrime of int;;
exception NotPrime of int
```

We have defined two exceptions – Problem, and NotPrime which carries an integer along with it. Exceptions must start with a capital letter. The **of** construct can be used to introduce the type of information

55

```
take : int → α list → α list
drop : int → α list → α list

let rec take n l =
  match l with
    [] ->
      if n = 0
        then []
        else raise (Invalid_argument "take")        note the parentheses
  | h::t ->
      if n < 0 then raise (Invalid_argument "take") else
        if n = 0 then [] else h :: take (n - 1) t

let rec drop n l =
  match l with
    [] ->
      if n = 0
        then []
        else raise (Invalid_argument "drop")
  | h::t ->
      if n < 0 then raise (Invalid_argument "drop") else
        if n = 0 then l else drop (n - 1) t
```

Figure 7.1: Adding exceptions to take and drop

which travels along with an exception. Once they are defined we may use them in our own functions, using **raise**:

```
        OCaml
```

```
# exception Problem;;
exception Problem
# let f x = if x < 0 then raise Problem else 100 / x;;
val f : int -> int = <fun>
# f 5
- : int = 20
# f (-1);;
Exception: Problem.
```

Exceptions can be *handled* as well as raised. An *exception handler* deals with an exception raised by an expression. Exception handlers are written using the **try** ... **with** construct:

```
safe_divide : int → int → int

let safe_divide x y =
  try x / y with
    Division_by_zero -> 0
```

The `safe_divide` function tries to divide x by y, but if the expression x / y raises the built-in exception `Division_by_zero`, instead we return zero. Thus, our `safe_divide` function succeeds for every argument.

How do the types work here? The expression x / y has type **int** and so the expression we substitute in case of `Division_by_zero` must have the same type: **int**, which indeed it does. And so, our rule that each expression must have one and only one type is not violated – `safe_divide` always returns an **int**.

$$\underbrace{\textbf{try}\ \overbrace{\text{x / y}}^{\text{int}}\ \textbf{with}\ \text{Division\_by\_zero} \rightarrow \overbrace{\text{0}}^{\text{int}}}_{\text{int}}$$

Here is another example. The function `last` returns the last element of a list:

```
last : α list → α

let rec last l =
  match l with
    [x] -> x
  | _::t -> last t
```

The pattern match is incomplete, so whilst OCaml accepts the program it can fail at run-time. We can tidy up the situation by raising the built-in exception `Not_found`:

```
last : α list → α

let rec last l =
  match l with
    [] -> raise Not_found
  | [x] -> x
  | _::t -> last t
```

The type of a function gives no indication of what exceptions it might raise or handle; it is the responsibility of the programmer to ensure that exceptions which should be handled always are – this is an area in which the type system cannot help us. Later in this book, we will see some alternatives to exceptions for occasions when they are likely to be frequently raised, allowing the type system to make sure we have dealt with each possible circumstance.

Questions

1. Write a function `smallest` which returns the smallest positive element of a list of integers. If there is no positive element, it should raise the built-in `Not_found` exception.

2. Write another function `smallest_or_zero` which uses the `smallest` function but if `Not_found` is raised, returns zero.

3. Write an exception definition and a function which calculates the largest integer smaller than or equal to the square root of a given integer. If the argument is negative, the exception should be raised.

4. Write another function which uses the previous one, but handles the exception, and simply returns zero when a suitable integer cannot be found.

5. Comment on the merits and demerits of exceptions as a method for dealing with exceptional situations, in contrast to returning a special value to indicate an error (such as -1 for a function normally returning a positive number).

So Far

1 Integers min_int ... -3 -2 -1 0 1 2 3 ... max_int of type **int**. Booleans true and false of type **bool**. Characters of type **char** like 'X' and '!'.

Mathematical operators + - * / mod which take two integers and give another.

Operators = < <= > >= <> which compare two values and evaluate to either true or false.

The conditional **if** *expression1* **then** *expression2* **else** *expression3*, where *expresssion1* has type **bool** and *expression2* and *expression3* have the same type as one another.

The boolean operators && and || which allow us to build compound boolean expressions.

2 Assigning a name to the result of evaluating an expression using the **let** *name* = *expression* construct. Building compound expressions using **let** *name1* = *expression1* **in** **let** *name2* = *expression2* **in** ...

Functions, introduced by **let** *name argument1 argument2* ... = *expression*. These have type $\alpha \to \beta$, $\alpha \to \beta \to \gamma$ etc. for some types α, β, γ etc.

Recursive functions, which are introduced in the same way, but using **let rec** instead of **let**.

3 Matching patterns using **match** *expression1* **with** *pattern1* | ... -> *expression2* | *pattern2* | ... -> *expression3* | ... The expressions *expression2*, *expression3* etc. must have the same type as one another, and this is the type of the whole **match ... with** expression.

4 Lists, which are ordered collections of zero or more elements of like type. They are written between square brackets, with elements separated by semicolons e.g. [1; 2; 3; 4; 5]. If a list is non-empty, it has a head, which is its first element, and a tail, which is the list composed of the rest of the elements.

The :: "cons" operator, which adds an element to the front of a list. The @ "append" operator, which concatenates two lists together.

Lists and the :: "cons" symbol may be used for pattern matching to distinguish lists of length zero, one, etc. and with particular contents.

5 Matching two or more things at once, using commas to separate as in **match** a, b **with** 0, 0 -> *expression1* | x, y -> *expression2* | ...

6 Anonymous functions **fun** *name* -> *expression*. Making operators into functions as in (<) and (+).

7 Defining exceptions with **exception** *name*. They can carry extra information by adding **of** *type*. Raising exceptions with **raise**. Handling exceptions with **try** ... **with** ...

Chapter 8

Looking Things Up

Many programs make use of a structure known as a *dictionary*. A real dictionary is used for associating definitions with words; we use "dictionary" more generally to mean associating some unique *keys* (like words) with *values* (like definitions). For example, we might like to store the following information about the number of people living in each house in a road:

House	People
1	4
2	2
3	2
4	3
5	1
6	2

The house number is the key, the number of people living in the house is the value. The order of keys is unimportant – we just need to be able to associate each key with one (and only one) value. It would be very inconvenient to store two lists, one of house numbers and one of people. For one thing, we would have way of guaranteeing the two lists were of equal length. What we would like is a way of representing pairs like (1, 4) and then having a single list of those. To make a pair in OCaml, just write it with parentheses and a comma:

```
p : int × int

let p = (1, 4)
```

It has the type **int** × **int**, which we pronounce as "int cross int". When printed on the screen, ∗ is used instead of × just as with multiplication. The two parts of the pair need not have the same type:

```
q : int × char

let q = (1, '1')
```

We can write simple functions to extract the first and second element using pattern matching:

```
fst : α × β → α
snd : α × β → β

let fst p = match p with (x, _) -> x
let snd p = match p with (_, y) -> y
```

In fact, since pairs can only take one form (unlike lists, which have two forms: empty or consisting of a head and a tail), OCaml lets us use the pattern directly in place of the argument:

```
fst : α × β → α
snd : α × β → β

let fst (x, _) = x
let snd (_, y) = y
```

Now, we can store a dictionary as a list of pairs:

```
census : (int × int) list

let census = [(1, 4); (2, 2); (3, 2); (4, 3); (5, 1); (6, 2)]
```

Notice the parentheses around **int** × **int** in the type. Otherwise, it would be the type of a pair of an integer and an integer list:

```
y : int × int list

let y = (1, [2; 3; 4])
```

What operations might we want on dictionaries? We certainly need to look up a value given a key:

```
lookup : α → (α × β) list → β

let rec lookup x l =
  match l with
    [] -> raise Not_found              we reached the end, and did not find it
  | (k, v)::t ->
      if k = x then v else lookup x t   return the value, or keep looking
```

For example, `lookup 4 census` evaluates to 3, whereas `lookup 9 census` raises `Not_found`. Another basic operation is to add an entry (we must replace it if it already exists, to maintain the property that each key appears at most once in a dictionary).

```
add : α → β → (α × β) list → (α × β) list

let rec add k v d =                              key, value, dictionary
  match d with
    [] -> [(k, v)]                               it is not present, so add it
  | (k', v')::t ->
      if k = k'
        then (k, v) :: t                   found an equal key so replace the entry
        else (k', v') :: add k v t          otherwise, keep the entry and continue
```

For example, `add 6 2 [(4, 5); (6, 3)]` evaluates to `[(4, 5); (6, 2)]` (the value for key 6 is replaced), whereas `add 6 2 [(4, 5); (3, 6)]` evaluates to `[(4, 5); (3, 6); (6, 2)]` (the new entry for key 6 is added). Removing an element is easy:

```
remove : α → (α × β) list → (α × β) list

let rec remove k d =
  match d with
    [] -> []                                it is not present, so we are done
  | (k', v')::t ->
      if k = k'
        then t                        equal key – remove it, and we are done
        else (k', v') :: remove k t        otherwise, retain and keep looking
```

The function always succeeds – even if the key was not found. We can use exception handling together with our lookup operation to build a function which checks if a key exists within a dictionary:

```
key_exists : α → (α × β) list → bool

let key_exists k d =
  try
    let _ = lookup k d in true
  with
    Not_found -> false
```

If `lookup k d` succeeds, `true` will be returned. If not, an exception will be raised, which `key_exists` will handle itself, and return `false`. Note that we did not give a name to the result of `lookup k l` because we always return `true` if it succeeds.

Pairs are just a particular instance of a more general construct – the *tuple*. A tuple may contain two or more things. For example, `(1, false, 'a')` has type **int** × **bool** × **char**.

Questions

1. Write a function to determine the number of different keys in a dictionary.

2. Define a function `replace` which is like add, but raises `Not_found` if the key is not already there.

3. Write a function to build a dictionary from two equal length lists, one containing keys and another containing values. Raise the exception `Invalid_argument` if the lists are not of equal length.

4. Now write the inverse function: given a dictionary, return the pair of two lists – the first containing all the keys, and the second containing all the values.

5. Define a function to turn any list of pairs into a dictionary. If duplicate keys are found, the value associated with the first occurrence of the key should be kept.

6. Write the function `union a b` which forms the union of two dictionaries. The union of two dictionaries is the dictionary containing all the entries in one or other or both. In the case that a key is contained in both dictionaries, the value in the first should be preferred.

So Far

1 Integers min_int ... -3 -2 -1 0 1 2 3 ... max_int of type **int**. Booleans true and false of type **bool**. Characters of type **char** like 'X' and '!'.

Mathematical operators + - * / mod which take two integers and give another.

Operators = < <= > >= <> which compare two values and evaluate to either true or false.

The conditional **if** *expression1* **then** *expression2* **else** *expression3*, where *expresssion1* has type **bool** and *expression2* and *expression3* have the same type as one another.

The boolean operators && and || which allow us to build compound boolean expressions.

2 Assigning a name to the result of evaluating an expression using the **let** *name* = *expression* construct. Building compound expressions using **let** *name1* = *expression1* **in** **let** *name2* = *expression2* **in** ...

Functions, introduced by **let** *name argument1 argument2* ... = *expression*. These have type $\alpha \to \beta, \alpha \to \beta \to \gamma$ etc. for some types α, β, γ etc.

Recursive functions, which are introduced in the same way, but using **let rec** instead of **let**.

3 Matching patterns using **match** *expression1* **with** *pattern1* | ... -> *expression2* | *pattern2* | ... -> *expression3* | ... The expressions *expression2, expression3* etc. must have the same type as one another, and this is the type of the whole **match ... with** expression.

4 Lists, which are ordered collections of zero or more elements of like type. They are written between square brackets, with elements separated by semicolons e.g. [1; 2; 3; 4; 5]. If a list is non-empty, it has a head, which is its first element, and a tail, which is the list composed of the rest of the elements.

The :: "cons" operator, which adds an element to the front of a list. The @ "append" operator, which concatenates two lists together.

Lists and the :: "cons" symbol may be used for pattern matching to distinguish lists of length zero, one, etc. and with particular contents.

5 Matching two or more things at once, using commas to separate as in **match** a, b **with** 0, 0 -> *expression1* | x, y -> *expression2* | ...

6 Anonymous functions **fun** *name* -> *expression*. Making operators into functions as in (<) and (+).

7 Defining exceptions with **exception** *name*. They can carry extra information by adding **of** *type*. Raising exceptions with **raise**. Handling exceptions with **try** ... **with** ...

8 Tuples to combine a fixed number of elements (a, b), (a, b, c) etc. with types $\alpha \times \beta$, $\alpha \times \beta \times \gamma$ etc.

Chapter 9

More with Functions

Look again at the type of a simple function with more than one argument:

```
add : int → int → int

let add x y = x + y
```

We have been considering functions like this as taking two arguments and returning a result. In fact, the truth is a little different. The type **int** → **int** → **int** can also be written as **int** → (**int** → **int**). OCaml lets us omit the parentheses because → is a right-associative operator in the language of types. This gives us a clue.

> *In truth, the function **add** is a function which, when you give it an integer, gives you a function which, when you give it an integer, gives the sum.*

This would be of no particular interest to us, except for one thing: we can give a function with two arguments just one argument at a time, and it turns out to be rather useful. For example:

OCaml

```
# let add x y = x + y
val add : int -> int -> int = <fun>
# let f = add 6
val f : int -> int = <fun>
# f 5
- : int = 11
```

Here, we have defined a function f by applying just one argument to add. This gives a function of type **int** → **int** which adds six to any number. We then apply 5 to this function, giving 11. When defining f, we used *partial application* (we applied only some of the arguments). In fact, even when applying all the arguments at once, we could equally write (add 6) 5 rather than add 6 5. We can add six to every element in a list:

```
map (add 6) [10; 20; 30]
```

Here, add 6 has the type **int** → **int**, which is an appropriate type to be the first argument to map when mapping over a list of integers. We can use partial application to simplify some examples from earlier in the book. We mentioned that you can write, for example, (*) to produce a function from an operator. It has type **int** → **int** → **int**. We may partially apply this function, so instead of writing

```
map (fun x -> x * 2) [10; 20; 30]
```

we may write

```
map (( * ) 2) [10; 20; 30]
```

Recall the function to map something over a list of lists from the questions to Chapter 6:

```
mapl : (α → β) → α list list → β list list

let rec mapl f l =
  match l with
    [] -> []
  | h::t -> map f h :: mapl f t
```

With partial application, we can write

```
mapl : (α → β) → α list list → β list list

let mapl f l = map (map f) l
```

Can you see why? The partially applied function map f is of type α **list** → β **list**, which is exactly the right type to pass to map when mapping over lists of lists. In fact, we can go even further and write:

```
mapl : (α → β) → α list list → β list list

let mapl f = map (map f)
```

Here, map (map f) has type α **list list** → β **list list** so when an f is supplied to mapl, a function is returned requiring just the list. This is partial application at work again.

You can see the real structure of multiple-argument functions, by writing add using anonymous functions:

```
add : int → int → int

let add = fun x -> fun y -> x + y
```

This makes it more obvious that our two-argument add function is really just composed of one-argument functions, but **let** add x y = x + y is much clearer! We can apply one or more arguments at a time, but they must be applied in order. Everything in this chapter also works for functions with more than two arguments.

SUMMARY

The function f x y has type $\alpha \to \beta \to \gamma$ which can also be written $\alpha \to (\beta \to \gamma)$. Thus, it takes an argument of type α and returns a function of type $\beta \to \gamma$ which, when you give it an argument of type β returns something of type γ. And so, we can apply just one argument to the function f (which is called partial application), or apply both at once. When we write **let** f x y = . . . this is just shorthand for **let** f = **fun** x -> **fun** y -> . . .

Questions

1. Rewrite the summary paragraph at the end of this chapter for the three argument function g a b c.

2. Recall the function member x l which determines if an element x is contained in a list l. What is its type? What is the type of member x? Use partial application to write a function member_all x ls which determines if an element is a member of all the lists in the list of lists ls.

3. Why can we not write a function to halve all the elements of a list like this: map ((/) 2) [10; 20; 30]? Write a suitable division function which can be partially applied in the manner we require.

4. Write a function mapll which maps a function over lists of lists of lists. You must not use the **let rec** construct. Is it possible to write a function which works like map, mapl, or mapll depending upon the list given to it?

5. Write a function truncate which takes an integer and a list of lists, and returns a list of lists, each of which has been truncated to the given length. If a list is shorter than the given length, it is unchanged. Make use of partial application.

6. Write a function which takes a list of lists of integers and returns the list composed of all the first elements of the lists. If a list is empty, a given number should be used in place of its first element.

So Far

1 Integers min_int ... -3 -2 -1 0 1 2 3 ... max_int of type **int**. Booleans true and false of type **bool**. Characters of type **char** like 'X' and '!'.

Mathematical operators + - * / mod which take two integers and give another.

Operators = < <= > >= <> which compare two values and evaluate to either true or false.

The conditional **if** *expression1* **then** *expression2* **else** *expression3*, where *expression1* has type **bool** and *expression2* and *expression3* have the same type as one another.

The boolean operators && and || which allow us to build compound boolean expressions.

2 Assigning a name to the result of evaluating an expression using the **let** *name* = *expression* construct. Building compound expressions using **let** *name1* = *expression1* **in** **let** *name2* = *expression2* **in** ...

Functions, introduced by **let** *name argument1 argument2* ... = *expression*. These have type $\alpha \to \beta$, $\alpha \to \beta \to \gamma$ etc. for some types α, β, γ etc.

Recursive functions, which are introduced in the same way, but using **let rec** instead of **let**.

3 Matching patterns using **match** *expression1* **with** *pattern1* | ... -> *expression2* | *pattern2* | ... -> *expression3* | ... The expressions *expression2*, *expression3* etc. must have the same type as one another, and this is the type of the whole **match ... with** expression.

4 Lists, which are ordered collections of zero or more elements of like type. They are written between square brackets, with elements separated by semicolons e.g. [1; 2; 3; 4; 5]. If a list is non-empty, it has a head, which is its first element, and a tail, which is the list composed of the rest of the elements.

The :: "cons" operator, which adds an element to the front of a list. The @ "append" operator, which concatenates two lists together.

Lists and the :: "cons" symbol may be used for pattern matching to distinguish lists of length zero, one, etc. and with particular contents.

5 Matching two or more things at once, using commas to separate as in **match** a, b **with** 0, 0 -> *expression1* | x, y -> *expression2* | ...

6 Anonymous functions **fun** *name* -> *expression*. Making operators into functions as in (<) and (+).

7 Defining exceptions with **exception** *name*. They can carry extra information by adding **of** *type*. Raising exceptions with **raise**. Handling exceptions with **try** ... **with** ...

8 Tuples to combine a fixed number of elements (a, b), (a, b, c) etc. with types $\alpha \times \beta$, $\alpha \times \beta \times \gamma$ etc.

9 Partial application of functions by giving fewer than the full number of arguments. Partial application with functions built from operators.

Chapter 10

New Kinds of Data

So far, we have considered the simple types **int**, **bool**, **char**, the compound type **list**, and tuples. We have built functions from and to these types. It would be possible to encode anything we wanted as lists and tuples of these types, but it would lead to complex and error-strewn programs. It is time to make our own types. New types are introduced using **type**. Here's a type for colours:

```
OCaml
```

```
# type colour = Red | Green | Blue | Yellow;;
type colour = Red | Green | Blue | Yellow
```

The name of our new type is colour. It has four *constructors*, written with an initial capital letter: Red, Green, Blue, and Yellow. These are the possible forms a value of type colour may take. Now we can build values of type colour:

```
col : colour
cols : colour list
colpair : char × colour

let col = Blue

let cols = [Red; Red; Green; Yellow]

let colpair = ('R', Red)
```

Let us extend our type to include any other colour which can be expressed in the RGB (Red, Green, Blue) colour system (each component ranges from 0 to 255 inclusive, a standard range giving about 16 million different colours).

```
type colour =
  Red
| Green
| Blue
| Yellow
| RGB of int × int × int

cols : colour list

let cols = [Red; Red; Green; Yellow; RGB (150, 0, 255)]
```

We use **of** in our new constructor, to carry information along with values built with it. Here, we are using something of type **int** × **int** × **int**. Notice that the list cols of type colour **list** contains varying things, but they are all of the same type, as required by a list. We can write functions by pattern matching over our new type:

```
components : colour → int × int × int

let components c =
  match c with
    Red -> (255, 0, 0)
  | Green -> (0, 255, 0)
  | Blue -> (0, 0, 255)
  | Yellow -> (255, 255, 0)
  | RGB (r, g, b) -> (r, g, b)
```

Types may contain a *type variable* like α to allow the type of part of the new type to vary – i.e. for the type to be polymorphic. For example, here is a type used to hold either nothing, or something of any type:

```
OCaml
```

```
# type 'a option = None | Some of 'a;;
type 'a option = None | Some of 'a
```

We can read this as "*a value of type α option is either nothing, or something of type α*". For example:

```
nothing : α option
number : int option
numbers : int option list
word : char list option

let nothing = None

let number = Some 50

let numbers = [Some 12; None; None; Some 2]

let word = Some ['c'; 'a'; 'k'; 'e']
```

The option type is useful as a more manageable alternative to exceptions where the lack of an answer is a common (rather than genuinely exceptional) occurrence. For example, here is a function to look up a value in a dictionary, returning None instead of raising an exception if the value is not found:

```
lookup_opt : α → (α × β) list → β option

let rec lookup_opt x l =
  match l with
    [] -> None
  | (k, v)::t -> if x = k then Some v else lookup_opt x t
```

Now, there is no need to worry about exception handling – we just pattern match on the result of the function.

In addition to being polymorphic, new types may also be recursively defined. We can use this functionality to define our own lists, just like the built-in lists in OCaml but without the special notation:

OCaml

```
# type 'a sequence = Nil | Cons of 'a * 'a sequence;;
type 'a sequence = Nil | Cons of 'a * 'a sequence
```

We have called our type sequence to avoid confusion. It has two constructors: Nil which is equivalent to [], and Cons which is equivalent to the :: operator. Cons carries two pieces of data with it – one of type α (the head) and one of type α sequence (the tail). This is the recursive part of our definition. Now we can make our own lists equivalent to OCaml's built-in ones:

Built-in	Ours	Our Type
[]	Nil	α sequence
[1]	Cons (1, Nil)	**int** sequence
['a'; 'x'; 'e']	Cons ('a', Cons ('x', Cons ('e', Nil)))	**char** sequence
[Red; RGB (20, 20, 20)]	Cons (Red, Cons (RGB (20, 20, 20), Nil))	colour sequence

Now you can see why getting at the last element of a list in OCaml is harder than getting at the first element – it is deeper in the structure. Let us compare some functions on OCaml lists with the same ones on our new sequence type. First, the ones for built-in lists.

```
length : α list → int
append : α list → α list → α list

let rec length l =
  match l with
    [] -> 0
  | _::t -> 1 + length t

let rec append a b =
  match a with
    [] -> b
  | h::t -> h :: append t b
```

And now the same functions with our new sequence type:

```
length : α sequence → int
append : α sequence → α sequence → α sequence

let rec length s =
  match s with
    Nil -> 0
  | Cons (_, t) -> 1 + length t

let rec append a b =
  match a with
    Nil -> b
  | Cons (h, t) -> Cons (h, append t b)
```

Notice how all the conveniences of pattern matching such as completeness detection and the use of the underscore work for our own types too.

A Type for Mathematical Expressions

Our sequence was an example of a recursively-defined type, which can be processed naturally by recursive functions. Mathematical expressions can be modeled in the same way. For example, the expression $1 + 2 \times 3$ could be drawn like this:

Notice that, in this representation, we never need parentheses – the diagram is unambiguous. We can evaluate the expression by reducing each part in turn:

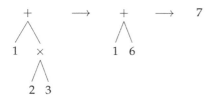

Here's a suitable type for such expressions:

```
type expr =
  Num of int
| Add of expr * expr
| Subtract of expr * expr
| Multiply of expr * expr
| Divide of expr * expr
```

For example, the expression $1 + 2 * 3$ is represented in this data type as:

```
Add (Num 1, Multiply (Num 2, Num 3))
```

We can now write a function to evaluate expressions:

```
evaluate : expr → int

let rec evaluate e =
  match e with
    Num x -> x
  | Add (e, e') -> evaluate e + evaluate e'
  | Subtract (e, e') -> evaluate e - evaluate e'
  | Multiply (e, e') -> evaluate e * evaluate e'
  | Divide (e, e') -> evaluate e / evaluate e'
```

Building our own types leads to clearer programs with more predictable behaviour, and helps us to think about a problem – often the functions are easy to write once we have decided on appropriate types.

Questions

1. Design a new type rect for representing rectangles. Treat squares as a special case.

2. Now write a function of type rect → **int** to calculate the area of a given rect.

3. Write a function which rotates a rect such that it is at least as tall as it is wide.

4. Use this function to write one which, given a rect **list**, returns another such list which has the smallest total width and whose members are sorted narrowest first.

5. Write take, drop, and map functions for the sequence type.

6. Extend the expr type and the evaluate function to allow raising a number to a power.

7. Use the option type to deal with the problem that Division_by_zero may be raised from the evaluate function.

So Far

1 Integers `min_int` ... `-3 -2 -1 0 1 2 3` ... `max_int` of type **int**. Booleans `true` and `false` of type **bool**. Characters of type **char** like `'X'` and `'!'`.

Mathematical operators `+ - * / mod` which take two integers and give another.

Operators `= < <= > >= <>` which compare two values and evaluate to either `true` or `false`.

The conditional **if** *expression1* **then** *expression2* **else** *expression3*, where *expresssion1* has type **bool** and *expression2* and *expression3* have the same type as one another.

The boolean operators `&&` and `||` which allow us to build compound boolean expressions.

2 Assigning a name to the result of evaluating an expression using the **let** *name* = *expression* construct. Building compound expressions using **let** *name1* = *expression1* **in** **let** *name2* = *expression2* **in** ...

Functions, introduced by **let** *name argument1 argument2* ... = *expression*. These have type $\alpha \rightarrow \beta, \alpha \rightarrow \beta \rightarrow \gamma$ etc. for some types α, β, γ etc.

Recursive functions, which are introduced in the same way, but using **let rec** instead of **let**.

3 Matching patterns using **match** *expression1* **with** *pattern1* | ... -> *expression2* | *pattern2* | ... -> *expression3* |... The expressions *expression2*, *expression3* etc. must have the same type as one another, and this is the type of the whole **match** ... **with** expression.

4 Lists, which are ordered collections of zero or more elements of like type. They are written between square brackets, with elements separated by semicolons e.g. `[1; 2; 3; 4; 5]`. If a list is non-empty, it has a head, which is its first element, and a tail, which is the list composed of the rest of the elements.

The `::` "cons" operator, which adds an element to the front of a list. The `@` "append" operator, which concatenates two lists together.

Lists and the `::` "cons" symbol may be used for pattern matching to distinguish lists of length zero, one, etc. and with particular contents.

5 Matching two or more things at once, using commas to separate as in **match** a, b **with** 0, 0 -> *expression1* | x, y -> *expression2* | ...

6 Anonymous functions **fun** *name* -> *expression*. Making operators into functions as in `( < )` and `( + )`.

7 Defining exceptions with **exception** *name*. They can carry extra information by adding **of** *type*. Raising exceptions with **raise**. Handling exceptions with **try** ... **with** ...

8 Tuples to combine a fixed number of elements (a, b), (a, b, c) etc. with types $\alpha \times \beta, \alpha \times \beta \times \gamma$ etc.

9 Partial application of functions by giving fewer than the full number of arguments. Partial application with functions built from operators.

10 New types with **type** *name* = *constructor1* **of** *type1* | *constructor2* **of** *type2* | ... Pattern matching on them as with the built-in types. Polymorphic types.

Chapter 11

Growing Trees

We have used lists to represent collections of elements of like type but varying length, and tuples to represent collections of things of any type but fixed length. Another common type is the *binary tree*, which is used to represent structures which branch, such as the arithmetical expressions we constructed in the last chapter.

How can we represent such trees using an OCaml type? When we built our version of the OCaml list type, we had two constructors – Cons to hold a head and a tail, and Nil to represent the end of the list. With a tree, we need a version of Cons which can hold two tails – the left and right, and we still need a version of Nil.

```
type 'a tree =
  Br of 'a * 'a tree * 'a tree                        branch
| Lf                                                    leaf
```

Our type is called tree, and is polymorphic (can hold any kind of data at the branches). There are two constructors: Br for branches, which hold three things in a tuple: an element, the left sub-tree, and the right sub-tree. If it is not a Br, it is a Lf (leaf), which is used to signal that there is no left, or no right sub-tree. Here are some representations in our new type of integer trees:

1
    is written as   Br (1, Lf, Lf)

2
    is written as   Br (2, Br (1, Lf, Lf), Lf)
1

```
2          is written as    Br (2, Br (1, Lf, Lf), Br (4, Lf, Lf))
```

The empty tree is simply `Lf`. You can see now why we used abbreviated constructor names – even small trees result in long textual representations. Let us write some simple functions on trees. To calculate the number of elements in the tree, we just count one for each branch, and zero for each leaf:

```
size : α tree → int

let rec size tr =
  match tr with
    Br (_, l, r) -> 1 + size l + size r
  | Lf -> 0
```

Notice that the recursive function follows the shape of the recursive type. A similar function can be used to add up all the integers in an **int** tree:

```
total : int tree → int

let rec total tr =
  match tr with
    Br (x, l, r) -> x + total l + total r
  | Lf -> 0
```

How can we calculate the maximum depth of a tree? The depth is the longest path from the root (top) of the tree to a leaf.

```
max : int → int → int
maxdepth : α tree → int

let max x y =
  if x > y then x else y

let rec maxdepth tr =
  match tr with
    Br (_, l, r) -> 1 + max (maxdepth l) (maxdepth r)
  | Lf -> 0
```

We defined a function `max` which returns the larger of two integers. Then, in our main function, we count a leaf as zero depth, and calculate the depth of a branch as one plus the maximum of the left and right sub-trees coming from that branch. Now consider extracting all of the elements from a tree into a list:

```
list_of_tree : α tree → α list

let rec list_of_tree tr =
  match tr with
    Br (x, l, r) -> list_of_tree l @ [x] @ list_of_tree r
  | Lf -> []
```

Notice that we chose to put all the elements on the left branch before the current element, and all the elements in the right branch after. This is arbitrary (it is clear that there are multiple answers to the question "How can I extract all the elements from a tree as a list?"). Before we consider real applications of trees, let us look at one more function. Here is how to map over trees:

```
tree_map : (α → β) → α tree → β tree

let rec tree_map f tr =
  match tr with
    Br (x, l, r) -> Br (f x, tree_map f l, tree_map f r)
  | Lf -> Lf
```

Notice the similarity to our map function for lists, both in the type and the definition.

Using trees to build better dictionaries

We have seen that arithmetic expressions can be drawn as trees on paper, and we have designed an OCaml data type for binary trees to hold any kind of element. Now it is time to introduce the most important application of trees: the *binary search tree*, which is another way of implementing the dictionary *data structure* we described in Chapter 8.

The most important advantage of a tree is that it is often very much easier to reach a given element. When searching in a dictionary defined as a list, it took on average time proportional to the number of items in the dictionary to find a value for a key (the position of the required entry is, on average, halfway along the list). If we use a binary tree, and if it is reasonably nicely balanced in shape, that time can be reduced to the logarithm base two of the number of elements in the dictionary. Can you see why?

We can use our existing tree type. In the case of a dictionary, it will have type $(\alpha \times \beta)$ tree, in other words a tree of key-value pairs where the keys have some type α and the values some type β. For this example, we are going to be using another built-in type, **string**. A string is a sequence of characters written between double quotation marks. We have seen these as messages attached to exceptions, but they are a basic OCaml type too.

So, our tree representing a dictionary mapping integers like **1** to their spellings like **"one"** would have type (**int** × **string**) tree:

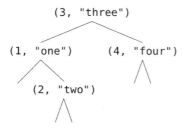

which would be written as

```
Br ((3, "three"), Br ((1, "one"), Lf, Br ((2, "two"), Lf, Lf)), Br ((4, "four"), Lf, Lf))
```

If we arrange the tree such that, at each branch, everything to the left has a key less than the key at the branch, and everything to the right has a key greater than that at the branch, we have a *binary search tree*.

Lookup is simple: start at the top, and if we have not found the key we are looking for, go left or right depending upon whether the required key is smaller or larger than the value at the current branch. If we reach a leaf, the key was not in the tree (assuming the tree is a well-formed binary search tree), and we raise an exception.

```
lookup : (α × β) tree → α → β

let rec lookup tr k =
  match tr with
    Lf -> raise Not_found
  | Br ((k', v), l, r) ->
      if k = k' then v                    found the key – return the value
      else if k < k' then lookup l k                            go left
      else lookup r k                                          go right
```

Alternatively, we may use the option type to avoid exceptions:

```
lookup : (α × β) tree → α → β option

let rec lookup tr k =
  match tr with
    Lf -> None
  | Br ((k', v), l, r) ->
      if k = k' then Some v               found the key – return the value
      else if k < k' then lookup l k                            go left
      else lookup r k                                          go right
```

How can we insert a new key-value pair into an existing tree? We can find the position to insert by using the same procedure as the lookup function – going left or right at each branch as appropriate. If we find an equal key, we put our new value there instead. Otherwise, we will end up at a leaf, and this is the insertion point – thus, if the key is not in the dictionary when `insert` is used, it will be added in place of an existing leaf.

```
insert : (α × β) tree → α → β → (α × β) tree

let rec insert tr k v =
  match tr with
    Lf -> Br ((k, v), Lf, Lf)                              insert at leaf
  | Br ((k', v'), l, r) ->
      if k = k' then Br ((k, v), l, r)                     replace value
      else if k < k' then Br ((k', v'), insert l k v, r)        go left
      else Br ((k', v'), l, insert r k v)                      go right
```

For example, if we wish to insert the value `"zero"` for the key `0` in the tree drawn above, we would obtain

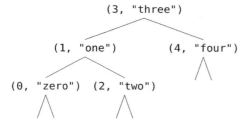

The shape of the tree is dependent upon the order of insertions into the tree – if they are in order (or reverse order), we obtain a rather inefficient tree – no better a dictionary than a list in fact. However, on average, we obtain a reasonably balanced tree, and logarithmic lookup and insertion times.

Lists and trees are examples of data structures. The design of an algorithm and its data structures are intimately connected.

Questions

1. Write a function of type $\alpha \rightarrow \alpha$ tree $\rightarrow$ **bool** to determine if a given element is in a tree.

2. Write a function which flips a tree left to right such that, if it were drawn on paper, it would appear to be a mirror image.

3. Write a function to determine if two trees have the same shape, irrespective of the actual values of the elements.

4. Write a function `tree_of_list` which builds a tree representation of a dictionary from a list representation of a dictionary.

5. Write a function to combine two dictionaries represented as trees into one. In the case of clashing keys, prefer the value from the first dictionary.

6. Can you define a type for trees which, instead of branching exactly two ways each time, can branch zero or more ways, possibly different at each branch? Write simple functions like `size`, `total`, and `map` using your new type of tree.

So Far

1 Integers `min_int` ... `-3 -2 -1 0 1 2 3` ... `max_int` of type **int**. Booleans `true` and `false` of type **bool**. Characters of type **char** like `'X'` and `'!'`.

Mathematical operators `+ - * / mod` which take two integers and give another.

Operators `= < <= > >= <>` which compare two values and evaluate to either `true` or `false`.

The conditional **if** *expression1* **then** *expression2* **else** *expression3*, where *expresssion1* has type **bool** and *expression2* and *expression3* have the same type as one another.

The boolean operators `&&` and `||` which allow us to build compound boolean expressions.

2 Assigning a name to the result of evaluating an expression using the **let** *name* = *expression* construct. Building compound expressions using **let** *name1* = *expression1* **in** **let** *name2* = *expression2* **in** ...

Functions, introduced by **let** *name argument1 argument2* ... = *expression*. These have type $\alpha \to \beta, \alpha \to \beta \to \gamma$ etc. for some types α, β, γ etc.

Recursive functions, which are introduced in the same way, but using **let rec** instead of **let**.

3 Matching patterns using **match** *expression1* **with** *pattern1* | ... -> *expression2* | *pattern2* | ... -> *expression3* | ... The expressions *expression2*, *expression3* etc. must have the same type as one another, and this is the type of the whole **match ... with** expression.

4 Lists, which are ordered collections of zero or more elements of like type. They are written between square brackets, with elements separated by semicolons e.g. `[1; 2; 3; 4; 5]`. If a list is non-empty, it has a head, which is its first element, and a tail, which is the list composed of the rest of the elements.

The `::` "cons" operator, which adds an element to the front of a list. The `@` "append" operator, which concatenates two lists together.

Lists and the `::` "cons" symbol may be used for pattern matching to distinguish lists of length zero, one, etc. and with particular contents.

5 Matching two or more things at once, using commas to separate as in **match** `a, b` **with** `0, 0` -> *expression1* | `x, y` -> *expression2* | ...

6 Anonymous functions **fun** *name* -> *expression*. Making operators into functions as in (<) and (+).

7 Defining exceptions with **exception** *name*. They can carry extra information by adding **of** *type*. Raising exceptions with **raise**. Handling exceptions with **try** ... **with** ...

8 Tuples to combine a fixed number of elements `(a, b)`, `(a, b, c)` etc. with types $\alpha \times \beta, \alpha \times \beta \times \gamma$ etc.

9 Partial application of functions by giving fewer than the full number of arguments. Partial application with functions built from operators.

10 New types with **type** *name* = *constructor1* **of** *type1* | *constructor2* **of** *type2* | ... Pattern matching on them as with the built-in types. Polymorphic types.

11 Strings, which are sequences of characters written between double quotes and are of type **string**.

Chapter 12

In and Out

We have considered a function (and indeed, a whole program composed of many functions) to take a chunk of data, do some calculations, and then produce a result. This assumption has allowed us to write neat, easily understood programs.

However, some computer programs do not have all data available at the beginning of the program (or even the beginning of a given function). The user might provide new data interactively, or the program might fetch data from the internet, or two or more programs might communicate with one another in real time.

We must learn how to write such programs, whilst understanding the utility of restricting such complications to as small a part of the program as possible – interactivity turns out to be surprisingly hard to reason about, since the result of a function may no longer depend only on its initial argument.

Writing to the screen

OCaml has a built-in function `print_int` which prints an integer to the screen:

```
OCaml
```

```
# print_int 100;;
100- : unit = ()
```

What is the type of this function? Well, it is a function, and it takes an integer as its argument. It prints the integer to the screen, and then returns. . . what? Nothing! OCaml has a special type to represent nothing, called **unit**. There is exactly one thing of type **unit** which is written () and is called "unit". So, the function `print_int` has type **int** → **unit**.

There is another built-in function `print_string` of type **string** → **unit** to print a string, and another `print_newline` to move to the next line. This function has type **unit** → **unit** because it requires no substantive argument and produces no useful result. It is only wanted for its "side-effect".

We can produce several side-effects, one after another, using the ; symbol. This evaluates the expression on its left hand side, throws away the result (which will normally be **unit** anyway), and then evaluates the expression to its right hand side, returning the result (which is often **unit** too). The type of the expression x ; y is thus the type of y. For example, we can write a function to write to the screen an **int** × **string** pair as an integer on one line, followed by a string on another:

```
print_dict_entry : int × string → unit

let print_dict_entry (k, v) =
  print_int k ; print_newline () ; print_string v ; print_newline ()
```

Notice we have added a second call to print_newline, so that our function can be called several times in a row without intervening calls to print_newline. We wrote the function applications all on one line to emphasize that ; behaves a little like an operator. However, for convenience, we would normally write it like this:

```
print_dict_entry : int × string → unit

let print_dict_entry (k, v) =
  print_int k;
  print_newline ();
  print_string v;
  print_newline ()
```

This makes it look rather like ; is used to end each expression, but just remember that ; is a bit like an operator – notice that there is no ; after the last print_newline (). Let us see how print_dict_entry is used in practice:

OCaml

```
# print_dict_entry (1, "one");;
1
one
- : unit = ()
```

How might we print a whole dictionary (represented as a list of entries) this way? Well, we could write our own function to iterate over all the entries:

```
print_dict : (int × string) list → unit

let rec print_dict d =
  match d with
    [] -> ()                                    do nothing; just return unit
  | h::t -> print_dict_entry h; print_dict t    do this one, and move on
```

Better, we can extract this method into a more general one, for doing an action on each element of a list:

```
iter : (α → β) → α list → unit

let rec iter f l =
  match l with
    [] -> ()                      do nothing; just return unit
  | h::t -> f h; iter f t         do this one, and move on
```

Normally β will be **unit**. Now we can redefine `print_dict` using `iter`:

```
print_dict : (int × string) list → unit

let print_dict d =
  iter print_dict_entry d

or even...

let print_dict =
  iter print_dict_entry
```

For example:

OCaml

```
# print_dict [(1, "one"); (2, "two"); (3, "three")];;
1
one
2
two
3
three
- : unit = ()
```

Reading from the keyboard

Now we should like to write a function to read a dictionary as an (**int** × **string**) **list**. We will use two built-in OCaml functions. The function `read_int` of type **unit** → **int** waits for the user to type in an integer and press the Enter key. The integer is then returned. The function `read_line` of type **unit** → **string** waits for the user to type any string and press the enter key, returning the string.

We want the user to enter a series of keys and values (integers and strings), one per line. They will enter zero for the integer to indicate no more input. Our function will take no argument, and return a dictionary of integers and strings, so its type will be **unit** → (**int** × **string**) **list**.

```
read_dict : unit → (int × string) list

let rec read_dict () =
  let i = read_int () in                    read an integer
    if i = 0 then [] else                   if zero, we are done
      let name = read_line () in            otherwise, read a name too
        (i, name) :: read_dict ()           build a dictionary entry, fetch another
```

We can run this function and type in some suitable values:

```
          OCaml
```

```
# read_dict ();;
1
oak
2
ash
3
elm
0
- : (int * string) list = [(1, "oak"); (2, "ash"); (3, "elm")]
```

But there is a problem. What happens if we type in something which is not an integer when an integer is
expected?

```
          OCaml
```

```
# read_dict ();;
1
oak
ash
Exception: Failure "int_of_string".
```

We must handle this exception, and ask the user to try again. Here's a revised function:

```
read_dict : unit → (int × string) list

let rec read_dict () =
  try
    let i = read_int () in                          read an integer
      if i = 0 then [] else                      if zero, we are done
        let name = read_line () in          otherwise, read a name too
          (i, name) :: read_dict ()    build a dictionary entry, fetch another
  with
    Failure "int_of_string" ->
      print_string "This is not a valid integer. Please try again.";
      print_newline ();
      read_dict ()
```

Now, typing mistakes can be fixed interactively:

```
          OCaml
```

```
# read_dict ();;
1
oak
ash
This is not a valid integer. Please try again.
```

```
2
ash
3
elm
0
- : (int * string) list = [(1, "oak"); (2, "ash"); (3, "elm")]
```

Using files

It is inconvenient to have to type new data sets in each time, so we will write functions to store a dictionary to a file, and then to read it back out again.

OCaml has some basic functions to help us read and write from places data can be stored, such as files. Places we can read from have type **in_channel** and places we can write to have type **out_channel**. Here are functions for writing a dictionary of type (**int** × **string**) to a channel:

```
entry_to_channel : out_channel → (int × string) → unit
dictionary_to_channel : out_channel → (int × string) list → unit

let entry_to_channel ch (k, v) =
  output_string ch (string_of_int k);
  output_char ch '\n';
  output_string ch v;
  output_char ch '\n'

let dictionary_to_channel ch d =
  iter (entry_to_channel ch) d
```

We are using the functions output_string and output_char to write the data in the same format we used to print it to the screen. There is no output_int function, so we have used the built-in string_of_int function to build a string from the integer. The character '\n' is a special one, representing moving to the next line (there is no output_newline function).

How do we obtain such a channel? The function open_out gives an output channel for filename given as a string. It has type **string** → **out_channel**. After we have written the contents to the file, we must call close_out (which has type **out_channel** → **unit**) to properly close the file.

```
dictionary_to_file : string → (int × string) list → unit

let dictionary_to_file filename dict =
  let ch = open_out filename in
    dictionary_to_channel ch dict;
    close_out ch
```

After running this function, you should find a file of the chosen name on your computer in the same folder from which you are running OCaml. If you are not sure where the file is being put, consult the documentation for your OCaml implementation, or use a full file path such as "C:/file.txt" or "/home/yourname/file.txt", again depending on your system. In the following example, we are reading a dictionary from the user and writing it to file as file.txt:

OCaml

```
# dictionary_to_file "file.txt" (read_dict ());;
1
oak
2
ash
3
elm
0
- : unit
```

Now we have written a file, we can read it back in:

```
entry_of_channel : in_channel → (int × string)
dictionary_of_channel : in_channel → (int × string) list

let entry_of_channel ch =
  let number = input_line ch in
    let name = input_line ch in
      (int_of_string number, name)

let rec dictionary_of_channel ch =
  try
    let e = entry_of_channel ch in
      e :: dictionary_of_channel ch
  with
    End_of_file -> []
```

We have written a function entry_of_channel to read a single integer and string (one element of our dictionary) from an input channel using the built-in functions input_line and int_of_string, and a function dictionary_of_channel to read all of them as a dictionary. It makes use of the built-in exception End_of_file to detect when there is no more in the file. Now, we can build the main function to read our dictionary from the file:

```
dictionary_of_file : string → (int × string) list

let dictionary_of_file filename =
  let ch = open_in filename in
    let dict = dictionary_of_channel ch in
      close_in ch;
      dict
```

The process is the same as for dictionary_to_file but we use open_in and close_in instead of open_out and close_out.

```
        OCaml
```

```
# dictionary_of_file "file.txt";;
- : (int * string) list = [(1, "oak"); (2, "ash"); (3, "elm")]
```

Summary of functions

We have introduced the types **unit**, **in_channel**, and **out_channel**, and the exception End_of_file. Here are the functions we have used:

Function	Type	Description
print_int	**int → unit**	Print an integer to the screen.
print_string	**string → unit**	Print a string to the screen.
print_newline	**unit → unit**	Print a newline character to the screen, moving to the beginning of the next line.
read_line	**unit → string**	Read a string from the user. The user indicates they have finished by pressing the Enter key.
read_int	**unit → int**	Read an integer from the user. The user indicates they have finished by pressing the Enter key. Raises Failure "int_of_string" if the user types something other than an integer.
int_of_string	**string → int**	Make an integer from a string. Raises Failure "int_of_string" if the string does not represent a valid integer.
string_of_int	**int → string**	Makes a string representation of an integer.
open_out	**string → out_channel**	Given a filename, open a channel for output. Raises the exception Sys_error if the file could not be opened.
close_out	**out_channel → unit**	Close an output channel.
open_in	**string → in_channel**	Given a filename, open a channel for input. Raises the exception Sys_error if the file could not be opened.
close_in	**in_channel → unit**	Close an input channel.
output_string	**out_channel → string → unit**	Write a string to an output channel.
output_char	**out_channel → char → unit**	Write a character to an output channel.

Questions

1. Write a function to print a list of integers to the screen in the same format OCaml uses – i.e. with square brackets and semicolons.

2. Write a function to read three integers from the user, and return them as a tuple. What exceptions could be raised in the process? Handle them appropriately.

3. In our `read_dict` function, we waited for the user to type 0 to indicate no more data. This is clumsy. Implement a new `read_dict` function with a nicer system. Be careful to deal with possible exceptions which may be raised.

4. Write a function which, given a number x, prints the x-times table to a given file name. For example, `table "table.txt" 5` should produce a file `table.txt` containing the following:

1	2	3	4	5
2	4	6	8	10
3	6	9	12	15
4	8	12	16	20
5	10	15	20	25

   Adding the special tabulation character `'\t'` after each number will line up the columns.

5. Write a function to count the number of lines in a given file.

6. Write a function `copy_file` of type **string** $\rightarrow$ **string** $\rightarrow$ **unit** which copies a file line by line. For example, `copy_file "a.txt" "b.txt"` should produce a file `b.txt` identical to `a.txt`. Make sure you deal with the case where the file `a.txt` cannot be found, or where `b.txt` cannot be created or filled.

So Far

1 Integers min_int ... -3 -2 -1 0 1 2 3 ... max_int of type **int**. Booleans true and false of type **bool**. Characters of type **char** like 'X' and '!'.

Mathematical operators + - * / mod which take two integers and give another.

Operators = < <= > >= <> which compare two values and evaluate to either true or false.

The conditional **if** *expression1* **then** *expression2* **else** *expression3*, where *expresssion1* has type **bool** and *expression2* and *expression3* have the same type as one another.

The boolean operators && and || which allow us to build compound boolean expressions.

2 Assigning a name to the result of evaluating an expression using the **let** *name* = *expression* construct. Building compound expressions using **let** *name1* = *expression1* **in** **let** *name2* = *expression2* **in** ...

Functions, introduced by **let** *name argument1 argument2* ... = *expression*. These have type $\alpha \rightarrow \beta, \alpha \rightarrow \beta \rightarrow \gamma$ etc. for some types α, β, γ etc.

Recursive functions, which are introduced in the same way, but using **let rec** instead of **let**.

3 Matching patterns using **match** *expression1* **with** *pattern1* | ... -> *expression2* | *pattern2* | ... -> *expression3* |... The expressions *expression2*, *expression3* etc. must have the same type as one another, and this is the type of the whole **match ... with** expression.

4 Lists, which are ordered collections of zero or more elements of like type. They are written between square brackets, with elements separated by semicolons e.g. [1; 2; 3; 4; 5]. If a list is non-empty, it has a head, which is its first element, and a tail, which is the list composed of the rest of the elements.

The :: "cons" operator, which adds an element to the front of a list. The @ "append" operator, which concatenates two lists together.

Lists and the :: "cons" symbol may be used for pattern matching to distinguish lists of length zero, one, etc. and with particular contents.

5 Matching two or more things at once, using commas to separate as in **match** a, b **with** 0, 0 -> *expression1* | x, y -> *expression2* | ...

6 Anonymous functions **fun** *name* -> *expression*. Making operators into functions as in (<) and (+).

7 Defining exceptions with **exception** *name*. They can carry extra information by adding **of** *type*. Raising exceptions with **raise**. Handling exceptions with **try** ... **with** ...

8 Tuples to combine a fixed number of elements (a, b), (a, b, c) etc. with types $\alpha \times \beta, \alpha \times \beta \times \gamma$ etc.

9 Partial application of functions by giving fewer than the full number of arguments. Partial application with functions built from operators.

10 New types with **type** *name* = *constructor1* **of** *type1* | *constructor2* **of** *type2* | ... Pattern matching on them as with the built-in types. Polymorphic types.

11 Strings, which are sequences of characters written between double quotes and are of type **string**.

12 The value () and its type **unit**. Input channels of type **in_channel** and output channels of type **out_channel**. Built-in functions for reading from and writing to them respectively.

Chapter 13

Putting Things in Boxes

So far, we have considered "pure" functions which have no side-effects, and functions which have the side-effect of reading or writing information to and from, for example, files. When we assigned a value to a name, that value could never change. Sometimes, it is convenient to allow the value of a name to be changed – some algorithms are more naturally expressed in this way.

OCaml provides a construct known as a *reference* which is a box in which we can store a value. We build a reference using the built-in function ref of type $\alpha \rightarrow \alpha$ **ref**. For example, let us build a reference with initial contents 0. It will have type **int ref**.

```
        OCaml

# let x = ref 0;;
val x : int ref = {contents = 0}
```

OCaml tells us that x is a reference of type **int ref** which currently has contents 0. We can extract the current contents of a reference using the ! operator, which has type α **ref** $\rightarrow \alpha$.

```
# let p = !x;;
val p : int = 0
```

We can update the contents of the reference using the := operator:

```
# x := 50;;
- : unit = ()
```

The := operator has type α **ref** $\rightarrow \alpha \rightarrow$ **unit**, since it takes a reference and a new value to put in it, puts the value in, and returns nothing. It is only useful for its side-effect. Now, we can get the contents with ! again.

```
# let q = !x;;
val q : int = 50
# p;;
- : int = 0
```

Notice that p is unchanged. Here's a function to swap the contents of two references:

99

```
swap : α ref → α ref → unit

let swap a b =
  let t = !a in
    a := !b; b := t
```

We needed to use a temporary name t to store the contents of a. Can you see why?

This type of programming, which consists of issuing a number of commands, in order, about which references are to be altered and how, is known as *imperative programming*. OCaml provides some useful structures for imperative programming with references. We will look at these quickly now, and in a moment build a bigger example program to show why they are useful.

For readability, OCaml lets us miss out the **else** part of the **if ... then ... else ...** construct if it would just be ( ), which is if we are doing nothing in the **else** case, so

```
if x = 0 then a := 0 else ()
```

can be written as

```
if x = 0 then a := 0
```

and if x is not zero, the expression will just evaluate to ( ). Due to this, when putting imperative code inside **if ... then ... else ...** constructs, we need to surround the inner imperative expressions with parentheses so the meaning is unambiguous:

```
if x = y then
  (a := !a + 1;
   b := !b - 1)
else
  c := !c + 1
```

OCaml allows us to use **begin** and **end** instead, for readability:

```
if x = y then
  begin
    a := !a + 1;
    b := !b - 1
  end
else
  c := !c + 1
```

Doing it again and again

There are two ways to repeat an action. To perform an action a fixed number of times, we use the **for ... = ... to ... do ... done** construct. For example,

```
    for x = 1 to 5 do print_int x; print_newline () done
```

evaluates the expression `print_int x; print_newline ()` five times: once where x is 1, once where x is 2 etc, so the result is:

```
# for x = 1 to 5 do print_int x; print_newline () done;
1
2
3
4
5
- : unit = ()
```

This is known as a "for loop". Note that the type of the whole **for** ... = ... **to** ... **do** ... **done** expression is **unit** irrespective of the type of the expression(s) inside it.

There is another looping construct – this time for evaluating an expression repeatedly until some condition is true. This is the **while** ... **do** ... **done** construct. It takes a boolean condition, and evaluates a given expression repeatedly, zero or more times, until the boolean condition is `false`. For example, here is a function which, given a positive integer, calculates the lowest power of two greater than or equal to that number (i.e. for the argument 37, the result will be 64).

```
smallest_pow2 : int → int

let smallest_pow2 x =                        
  let t = ref 1 in          start the test value at 1
    while !t < x do         each time it is less than x...
      t := !t * 2                     ...double it
    done;
    !t                  the final result is the contents of t
```

The **while** loop continues until the contents of the reference t is greater than or equal to x. At that point, it ends, and the contents of t is returned from the function. Again, note that the type of the whole **while** ... **do** ... **done** construct is **unit**.

Example: text file statistics

We are going to write a program to count the number of words, sentences and lines in a text file. We shall consider the opening paragraph of Kafka's "Metamorphosis".

```
One morning, when Gregor Samsa woke from troubled dreams, he found
himself transformed in his bed into a horrible vermin.  He lay on
his armour-like back, and if he lifted his head a little he could
see his brown belly, slightly domed and divided by arches into stiff
sections.  The bedding was hardly able to cover it and seemed ready
to slide off any moment.  His many legs, pitifully thin compared
with the size of the rest of him, waved about helplessly as he
looked.
```

There are newline characters at the end of each line, save for the last. You can cut and paste or type this into a text file to try these examples out. Here, it is saved as `gregor.txt`.

We will just count lines first. To this, we will write a function `channel_statistics` to gather the statistics by reading an input channel and printing them. Then we will have a function to open a named file, call our first function, and close it again.

```
channel_statistics : in_channel → unit
file_statistics : string → unit

let channel_statistics in_channel =
  let lines = ref 0 in
    try
      while true do
        let line = input_line in_channel in
          lines := !lines + 1
      done
    with
      End_of_file ->
        print_string "There were ";
        print_int !lines;
        print_string " lines.";
        print_newline ()

let file_statistics name =
  let channel = open_in name in
    try
      channel_statistics channel;
      close_in channel
    with
      _ -> close_in channel
```

Notice the use of `true` as the condition for the **while** construct. This means the computation would carry on forever, except that the `End_of_file` exception must eventually be raised. Note also that OCaml emits a warning when reading the `channel_statistics` function:

```
Warning 26: unused variable line.
```

This is an example of a warning we can ignore – we are not using the actual value `line` yet, since we are just counting lines without looking at their content. Running our program on the example file gives this:

```
            OCaml
```

```
# file_statistics "gregor.txt";;
There were 8 lines.
- : unit = ()
```

Let us update the program to count the number of words, characters, and sentences. We will do this simplistically, assuming that the number of words can be counted by counting the number of spaces, and that the sentences can be counted by noting instances of '.', '!', and '?'. We can extend the channel_statistics function appropriately – file_statistics need not change:

```
channel_statistics : in_channel → unit

let channel_statistics in_channel =
  let lines = ref 0 in
  let characters = ref 0 in
  let words = ref 0 in
  let sentences = ref 0 in
    try
      while true do
        let line = input_line in_channel in
          lines := !lines + 1;
          characters := !characters + String.length line;
          String.iter
            (fun c ->
              match c with
                '.' | '?' | '!' -> sentences := !sentences + 1
              | ' ' -> words := !words + 1
              | _ -> ())
            line
      done
    with
      End_of_file ->
        print_string "There were ";
        print_int !lines;
        print_string " lines, making up ";
        print_int !characters;
        print_string " characters with ";
        print_int !words;
        print_string " words in ";
        print_int !sentences;
        print_string " sentences.";
        print_newline ()
```

We have used the built-in function String.iter of type (**char** → **unit**) → **string** → **unit** which calls a function we supply on each character of a string.

Substituting this version of channel_statistics (if you are cutting and pasting into OCaml, be sure to also paste file_statistics in again afterwards, so it uses the new channel_statistics), gives the following result on our example text:

OCaml

```
# file_statistics "gregor.txt";;
There were 8 lines, making up 464 characters with 80 words in 4 sentences.
- : unit = ()
```

Adding character counts

We should like to build a histogram, counting the number of times each letter of the alphabet or other character occurs. It would be tedious and unwieldy to hold a hundred or so references, and then pattern match on each possible character to increment the right one. OCaml provides a data type called **array** for situations like this.

An array is a place for storing a fixed number of elements of like type. We can introduce arrays by using [| and |], with semicolons to separate the elements:

OCaml

```
# let a = [|1; 2; 3; 4; 5|];;
val a : int array = [|1; 2; 3; 4; 5|]
```

We can access an element inside our array in constant time by giving the position of the element (known as the *subscript*) in parentheses, after the array name and a period:

```
# a.(0);;
- : int = 1
```

Notice that the first element has subscript 0, not 1. We can update any of the values in the array, also in constant time, like this:

```
# a.(4) <- 100;;
- : unit = ()
# a;;
a : int array = [|1; 2; 3; 4; 100|]
```

If we try to access or update an element which is not within range, an exception is raised:

```
# a.(5);;
Exception: Invalid_argument "index out of bounds".
```

There are some useful built-in functions for dealing with arrays. The function `Array.length` of type α **array** $\rightarrow$ **int** returns the length of an array:

```
# Array.length a;;
- : int = 5
```

In contrast to finding the length of a list, the time taken by `Array.length` is constant, since it was fixed when the array was created. The `Array.make` function is used for building an array of a given length, initialized with given values. It takes two arguments – the length, and the initial value to be given to every element. It has type **int** $\rightarrow$ α $\rightarrow$ α **array**.

```
# Array.make 6 true;;
- : bool array = [|true; true; true; true; true; true|]
# Array.make 10 'A';;
- : char array = [|'A'; 'A'; 'A'; 'A'; 'A'; 'A'; 'A'; 'A'; 'A'; 'A'|]
# Array.make 3 (Array.make 3 5);;
- : int array array = [|[|5; 5; 5|]; [|5; 5; 5|]; [|5; 5; 5|]|]
```

Back to our original problem. We want to store a count for each possible character. We cannot subscript our arrays with characters directly, but each character has a special integer code (its so-called "ASCII code", a common encoding of characters as integers in use since the 1960s), and we can convert to and from these using the built-in functions int_of_char and char_of_int. For example:

OCaml

```
# int_of_char 'C';;
- : int = 67
# char_of_int 67;;
- : char = 'C'
```

The numbers go from 0 to 255 inclusive (they do not all represent printable characters, for example the newline character '\n' has code 10). So, we can store our histogram as an integer array of length 256.

Our main function is getting rather long, so we will write a separate one which, given the completed array prints out the frequencies. If there were no instances of a particular character, no line is printed for that character.

```
print_histogram : int array → unit

let print_histogram arr =
  print_string "Character frequencies:";
  print_newline ();
  for x = 0 to 255 do                                    for each character
    if arr.(x) > 0 then                          only if the count is non-zero
      begin
        print_string "For character '";
        print_char (char_of_int x);                       print the character
        print_string "'(character number ";
        print_int x;                                 print the character number
        print_string ") the count is ";
        print_int arr.(x);                                      print the count
        print_string ".";
        print_newline ()
      end
  done
```

This prints lines like:

```
For character 'd' (character number 100) the count is 6.
```

Now, we can alter our channel_statistics to create an appropriate array, and update it, once again using String.iter:

```
channel_statistics : in_channel → unit

let channel_statistics in_channel =
  let lines = ref 0 in
  let characters = ref 0 in          we do not indent all these lets.
  let words = ref 0 in
  let sentences = ref 0 in
  let histogram = Array.make 256 0 in      length 256, all elements initially 0
    try
      while true do
        let line = input_line in_channel in
          lines := !lines + 1;
          characters := !characters + String.length line;
          String.iter
            (fun c ->
              match c with
                '.' | '?' | '!' -> sentences := !sentences + 1
              | ' ' -> words := !words + 1
              | _ -> ())
            line;
          String.iter                         for each character...
            (fun c ->
              let i = int_of_char c in
                histogram.(i) <- histogram.(i) + 1)      update histogram
            line
      done
    with
      End_of_file ->
        print_string "There were ";
        print_int !lines;
        print_string " lines, making up ";
        print_int !characters;
        print_string " characters with ";
        print_int !words;
        print_string " words in ";
        print_int !sentences;
        print_string " sentences.";
        print_newline ();
        print_histogram histogram             call histogram printer
```

Here is the output on our text:

OCaml

```
# file_statistics "gregor.txt";;
There were 8 lines, making up 464 characters with 80 words in 4 sentences.
Character frequencies:
For character ' ' (character number 32) the count is 80.
For character ',' (character number 44) the count is 6.
For character '-' (character number 45) the count is 1.
```

```
For character '.' (character number 46) the count is 4.
For character 'G' (character number 71) the count is 1.
For character 'H' (character number 72) the count is 2.
For character 'O' (character number 79) the count is 1.
For character 'S' (character number 83) the count is 1.
For character 'T' (character number 84) the count is 1.
For character 'a' (character number 97) the count is 24.
For character 'b' (character number 98) the count is 10.
For character 'c' (character number 99) the count is 6.
For character 'd' (character number 100) the count is 25.
For character 'e' (character number 101) the count is 47.
For character 'f' (character number 102) the count is 13.
For character 'g' (character number 103) the count is 5.
For character 'h' (character number 104) the count is 22.
For character 'i' (character number 105) the count is 30.
For character 'k' (character number 107) the count is 4.
For character 'l' (character number 108) the count is 23.
For character 'm' (character number 109) the count is 15.
For character 'n' (character number 110) the count is 21.
For character 'o' (character number 111) the count is 27.
For character 'p' (character number 112) the count is 3.
For character 'r' (character number 114) the count is 20.
For character 's' (character number 115) the count is 24.
For character 't' (character number 116) the count is 21.
For character 'u' (character number 117) the count is 6.
For character 'v' (character number 118) the count is 4.
For character 'w' (character number 119) the count is 6.
For character 'y' (character number 121) the count is 10.
For character 'z' (character number 122) the count is 1.
- : unit = ()
```

The most common character is the space. The most common alphabetic character is 'e'.

Questions

1. Consider the expression
   let x = ref 1 **in let** y = ref 2 **in** x := !x + !x; y := !x + !y; !x + !y
   What references have been created? What are their initial and final values after this expression has been evaluated? What is the type of this expression?

2. What is the difference between [ref 5; ref 5] and **let** x = ref 5 **in** [x; x]?

3. Imagine that the **for ... to ... do ... done** construct did not exist. How might we create the same behaviour?

4. What are the types of these expressions?
   ```
   [|1; 2; 3|]
   [|true; false; true|]
   [|[|1|]|]
   [|[1; 2; 3]; [4; 5; 6]|]
   [|1; 2; 3|].(2)
   [|1; 2; 3|].(2) <- 4
   ```

5. Write a function to compute the sum of the elements in an integer array.

6. Write a function to reverse the elements of an array in place (i.e. do not create a new array).

7. Write a function **table** which, given an integer, builds the **int array array** representing the multiplication table up to that number. For example, **table 5** should yield:

1	2	3	4	5
2	4	6	8	10
3	6	9	12	15
4	8	12	16	20
5	10	15	20	25

   There is more than one way to represent this as an array of arrays; you may choose.

8. The ASCII codes for the lower case letters 'a'...'z' are 97...122, and for the upper case letters 'A'...'Z' they are 65...90. Use the built-in functions int_of_char and char_of_int to write functions to uppercase and lowercase a character. Non-alphabetic characters should remain unaltered.

9. Comment on the accuracy of our character, word, line, and sentence statistics in the case of our example paragraph. What about in general?

10. Choose one of the problems you have identified, and modify our program to fix it.

So Far

1 Integers min_int ... -3 -2 -1 0 1 2 3 ... max_int of type **int**. Booleans true and false of type **bool**. Characters of type **char** like 'X' and '!'.

Mathematical operators + - * / mod which take two integers and give another.

Operators = < <= > >= <> which compare two values and evaluate to either true or false.

The conditional **if** *expression1* **then** *expression2* **else** *expression3*, where *expresssion1* has type **bool** and *expression2* and *expression3* have the same type as one another.

The boolean operators && and || which allow us to build compound boolean expressions.

2 Assigning a name to the result of evaluating an expression using the **let** *name* = *expression* construct. Building compound expressions using **let** *name1* = *expression1* **in** **let** *name2* = *expression2* **in** ...

Functions, introduced by **let** *name argument1 argument2* ... = *expression*. These have type $\alpha \to \beta$, $\alpha \to \beta \to \gamma$ etc. for some types α, β, γ etc.

Recursive functions, which are introduced in the same way, but using **let rec** instead of **let**.

3 Matching patterns using **match** *expression1* **with** *pattern1* | ... -> *expression2* | *pattern2* | ... -> *expression3* | ... The expressions *expression2*, *expression3* etc. must have the same type as one another, and this is the type of the whole **match ... with** expression.

4 Lists, which are ordered collections of zero or more elements of like type. They are written between square brackets, with elements separated by semicolons e.g. [1; 2; 3; 4; 5]. If a list is non-empty, it has a head, which is its first element, and a tail, which is the list composed of the rest of the elements.

The :: "cons" operator, which adds an element to the front of a list. The @ "append" operator, which concatenates two lists together.

Lists and the :: "cons" symbol may be used for pattern matching to distinguish lists of length zero, one, etc. and with particular contents.

5 Matching two or more things at once, using commas to separate as in **match** a, b **with** 0, 0 -> *expression1* | x, y -> *expression2* | ...

6 Anonymous functions **fun** *name* -> *expression*. Making operators into functions as in (<) and (+).

7 Defining exceptions with **exception** *name*. They can carry extra information by adding **of** *type*. Raising exceptions with **raise**. Handling exceptions with **try** ... **with** ...

8 Tuples to combine a fixed number of elements (a, b), (a, b, c) etc. with types $\alpha \times \beta$, $\alpha \times \beta \times \gamma$ etc.

9 Partial application of functions by giving fewer than the full number of arguments. Partial application with functions built from operators.

10 New types with **type** *name* = *constructor1* **of** *type1* | *constructor2* **of** *type2* | ... Pattern matching on them as with the built-in types. Polymorphic types.

11 Strings, which are sequences of characters written between double quotes and are of type **string**.

12 The value () and its type **unit**. Input channels of type **in_channel** and output channels of type **out_channel**. Built-in functions for reading from and writing to them respectively.

13 References of type α **ref**. Building them using ref, accessing their contents using ! and updating them using the := operator.

Bracketing expressions together with **begin** and **end** instead of parentheses for readability.

Performing an action many times based on a boolean condition with the **while** *boolean expression* **do** *expression* **done** construct. Performing an action a fixed number of times with a varying parameter using the **for** *name* = *start* **to** *end* **do** *expression* **done** construct.

Arrays of type α **array**. Creating an array with the built-in function Array.make, finding its length with Array.length, accessing an element with a.(*subscript*). Updating with a.(*subscript*) <- *expression*. The built-in function String.iter.

Chapter 14

The Other Numbers

The only numbers we have considered until now have been the integers. For a lot of programming tasks, they are sufficient. And, except for their limited range and the possibility of division by zero, they are easy to understand and use. However, we must now consider the real numbers.

It is clearly not possible to represent all numbers exactly – they might be irrational like π or e and have no finite representation. For most uses, a representation called *floating-point* is suitable, and this is how OCaml's real numbers are stored. Not all numbers can be represented exactly, but arithmetic operations are very quick.

Floating-point numbers have type **float**. We can write a floating-point number by including a decimal point somewhere in it. For example 1.6 or 2. or 386.54123. Negative floating-point numbers are preceded by the -. characters just like negative integers are preceded by the - character. Similarly, we write +. -. *. /. for the standard arithmetic operators on floating-point numbers. Exponentiation is written with the ** operator.

```
      OCaml

# 1.5;;
- : float = 1.5
# 6.;;
- : float = 6.
# -.2.3456;;
- : float = -2.3456
# 1.0 +. 2.5 *. 3.0;;
- : float = 8.5
# 1.0 /. 1000.0;;
- : float = 0.001
# 1. /. 100000.;;
- : float = 1e-05
# 3000. ** 10.;;
- : float = 5.9049e+34
# 3.123 -. 3.;;
- : float = 0.12300000000000022
```

Notice an example of the limits of precision in floating-point operations in the final lines. Note also that very small or very large numbers are written using scientific notation (such as 5.9049e+34 above). We can find out the range of numbers available:

```
        OCaml

# max_float;;
- : float = 1.79769313486231571e+308
# min_float;;
- : float = 2.22507385850720138e-308
```

Working with floating-point numbers requires care, and a comprehensive discussion is outside the scope of this book. These challenges exist in any programming language using the floating-point system. For example, evaluating 1. /. 0. gives the special value infinity (there is no Division_by_zero exception for floating-point operations). There are other special values such as neg_infinity and nan ("not a number"). We will leave these complications for now – just be aware that they are lurking and must be confronted when writing robust numerical programs.

A number of standard functions are provided, both for operating on floating-point numbers and for converting to and from them, some of which are listed here:

Function	Type	Description
sqrt	**float** → **float**	Square root of a number.
log	**float** → **float**	Natural logarithm.
log10	**float** → **float**	Logarithm base ten.
sin	**float** → **float**	Sine of an angle, given in radians.
cos	**float** → **float**	Cosine of an angle, given in radians.
tan	**float** → **float**	Tangent of an angle, given in radians.
atan	**float** → **float**	Arctangent of an angle, given in radians.
ceil	**float** → **float**	Calculate the nearest whole number at least as big as a floating-point number.
floor	**float** → **float**	The nearest whole number at least as small as a floating-point number.
float_of_int	**int** → **float**	Convert an integer to a floating-point number.
int_of_float	**float** → **int**	Build an integer from a floating-point number, ignoring the non-integer part.
print_float	**float** → **unit**	Print a floating-point number to the screen.
string_of_float	**float** → **string**	Build a string from a floating-point number.
float_of_string	**string** → **float**	Build a floating-point number from a string. Raises Failure "float_of_string" on a bad argument.

Let us write some functions with floating-point numbers. We will write some simple operations on vectors in two dimensions. We will represent a point as a pair of floating-point numbers of type **float** × **float** such as (2.0, 3.0). We will represent a vector as a pair of floating-point numbers too. Now we can write a function to build a vector from one point to another, one to find the length of a vector, one to offset a point by a vector, and one to scale a vector to a given length:

```
make_vector : float × float → float × float → float × float
vector_length : float × float → float
offset_point : float × float → float × float → float × float
scale_to_length : float → float × float → float × float

let make_vector (x0, y0) (x1, y1) =
  (x1 -. x0, y1 -. y0)

let vector_length (x, y) =
  sqrt (x *. x +. y *. y)

let offset_point (x, y) (px, py) =
  (px +. x, py +. y)

let scale_to_length l (a, b) =
  let currentlength = vector_length (a, b) in
    if currentlength = 0. then (a, b) else      to avoid division by zero
      let factor = l /. currentlength in
        (a *. factor, b *. factor)
```

Notice that we have to be careful about division by zero, just as with integers. We have used tuples for the points because it is easier to read this way – we could have passed each floating-point number as a separate argument instead, of course.

Floating-point numbers are often essential, but must be used with caution. You will discover this when answering the questions for this chapter. Some of these questions require using the built-in functions listed in the table above.

Questions

1. Give a function which rounds a positive floating-point number to the nearest whole number, returning another floating-point number.

2. Write a function to find the point equidistant from two given points in two dimensions.

3. Write a function to separate a floating-point number into its whole and fractional parts. Return them as a tuple of type **float** × **float**.

4. Write a function star of type **float** → **unit** which, given a floating-point number between zero and one, draws an asterisk to indicate the position. An argument of zero will result in an asterisk in column one, and an argument of one an asterisk in column fifty.

5. Now write a function plot which, given a function of type **float** → **float**, a range, and a step size, uses star to draw a graph. For example, assuming the existence of the name pi for π, we might see:

```
OCaml

# plot sin 0. pi (pi /. 20.);;
*
        *
              *
                    *
                        *
                            *
                                *
                                    *
                                        *
                                            *
                                            *
                                            *
                                        *
                                    *
                                *
                            *
                        *
                    *
              *
        *
*
```

Here, we have plotted the sine function on the range $0 \ldots \pi$ in steps of size $\pi/20$. You can define *pi* by calculating 4.0 *. atan 1.0.

So Far

1 Integers `min_int` ... `-3 -2 -1 0 1 2 3` ... `max_int` of type **int**. Booleans `true` and `false` of type **bool**. Characters of type **char** like `'X'` and `'!'`.

Mathematical operators `+ - * / mod` which take two integers and give another.

Operators `= < <= > >= <>` which compare two values and evaluate to either `true` or `false`.

The conditional **if** *expression1* **then** *expression2* **else** *expression3*, where *expression1* has type **bool** and *expression2* and *expression3* have the same type as one another.

The boolean operators `&&` and `||` which allow us to build compound boolean expressions.

2 Assigning a name to the result of evaluating an expression using the **let** *name* = *expression* construct. Building compound expressions using **let** *name1* = *expression1* **in** **let** *name2* = *expression2* **in** ...

Functions, introduced by **let** *name argument1 argument2* ... = *expression*. These have type $\alpha \rightarrow \beta, \alpha \rightarrow \beta \rightarrow \gamma$ etc. for some types α, β, γ etc.

Recursive functions, which are introduced in the same way, but using **let rec** instead of **let**.

3 Matching patterns using **match** *expression1* **with** *pattern1* | ... -> *expression2* | *pattern2* | ... -> *expression3* |... The expressions *expression2*, *expression3* etc. must have the same type as one another, and this is the type of the whole **match** ... **with** expression.

4 Lists, which are ordered collections of zero or more elements of like type. They are written between square brackets, with elements separated by semicolons e.g. `[1; 2; 3; 4; 5]`. If a list is non-empty, it has a head, which is its first element, and a tail, which is the list composed of the rest of the elements.

The `::` "cons" operator, which adds an element to the front of a list. The `@` "append" operator, which concatenates two lists together.

Lists and the `::` "cons" symbol may be used for pattern matching to distinguish lists of length zero, one, etc. and with particular contents.

5 Matching two or more things at once, using commas to separate as in **match** a, b **with** 0, 0 -> *expression1* | x, y -> *expression2* | ...

6 Anonymous functions **fun** *name* -> *expression*. Making operators into functions as in (<) and (+).

7 Defining exceptions with **exception** *name*. They can carry extra information by adding **of** *type*. Raising exceptions with **raise**. Handling exceptions with **try** ... **with** ...

8 Tuples to combine a fixed number of elements (a, b), (a, b, c) etc. with types $\alpha \times \beta, \alpha \times \beta \times \gamma$ etc.

9 Partial application of functions by giving fewer than the full number of arguments. Partial application with functions built from operators.

10 New types with **type** *name* = *constructor1* **of** *type1* | *constructor2* **of** *type2* | ... Pattern matching on them as with the built-in types. Polymorphic types.

11 Strings, which are sequences of characters written between double quotes and are of type **string**.

12 The value ( ) and its type **unit**. Input channels of type **in_channel** and output channels of type **out_channel**. Built-in functions for reading from and writing to them respectively.

13 References of type α **ref**. Building them using `ref`, accessing their contents using `!` and updating them using the `:=` operator.

Bracketing expressions together with **begin** and **end** instead of parentheses for readability.

Performing an action many times based on a boolean condition with the **while** *boolean expression* **do** *expression* **done** construct. Performing an action a fixed number of times with a varying parameter using the **for** *name* = *start* **to** *end* **do** *expression* **done** construct.

Arrays of type α **array**. Creating an array with the built-in function `Array.make`, finding its length with `Array.length`, accessing an element with `a.(subscript)`. Updating with `a.(subscript) <- expression`. The built-in function `String.iter`.

14 Floating-point numbers `min_float` ... `max_float` of type **float**. Floating-point operators `+. *. -. /.` `**` and built-in functions `sqrt log` etc.

Chapter 15

The OCaml Standard Library

OCaml is provided with a wide range of useful built-in functions, in addition to the ones we have already seen, called the *OCaml Standard Library*. These functions are divided into *modules*, one for each area of functionality (in the next chapter, we will learn how to write our own modules). Here are a few examples of modules in the standard library:

List	The List module provides many functions over lists, some of which we have already written ourselves in earlier chapters. It also provides a simple implementation of dictionaries, and list sorting and searching functions.
Array	Functions for creating and modifying arrays, conversion to and from lists, and array sorting. Functions to iterate over arrays.
Char	Operations on characters, including conversions between characters and their integer equivalents.
String	Functions to build strings, together with searching, mapping, and iteration functions.
Random	Generating pseudo-random integers and floating-point numbers.
Buffer	Buffers are used for building strings up from sub-strings or characters, without the cost of repeated string concatenation.
Printf	Functions for printing with "format strings", which are more flexible and concise than repeated use of print_int and print_string etc.

We will take the List module as an example. You can find the documentation for the OCaml Standard Library installed with your copy of OCaml, or on the internet.

The functions from a module can be used by putting a period (full stop) between the module name and the function. For example the length function in the List module can be used like this:

```
OCaml
```

```
# List.length [1; 2; 3; 4; 5];;
- : int = 5
```

We can look at the type too by writing just the name of the function:

        OCaml

```
# List.length;;
- : 'a list -> int = <fun>
```

Here's the documentation for `List.length`:

> `val length : 'a list -> int`
>
>   Return the length (number of elements) of the given list.

We will talk about **val** in the next chapter. Sometimes, more information is required:

> `val nth : 'a list -> int -> 'a`
>
>   Return the n-th element of the list. The first element (head of the list) is at position 0.
>   Raise `Failure` `"nth"` if the list is too short. Raise `Invalid_argument` `"List.nth"` if n
>   is negative.

For example,

        OCaml

```
# List.nth [1; 2; 4; 8; 16] 3;;
- : int = 8
```

In the documentation, we are told what the function does for each argument, and what exceptions may be raised. Functions which are not tail-recursive and so may fail on huge arguments are marked as such.

    The questions for this chapter use functions from the standard library, so you will need to have a copy of the documentation to hand.

Questions

1. Write your own version of the function `List.concat`. The implementation OCaml provides is not tail-recursive. Can you write one which is?

2. Use `List.mem` to write a function which returns `true` only if every list in a **bool list list** contains `true` somewhere in it.

3. Write a function to count the number of exclamation marks in a string, using one or more functions from the `String` module.

4. Use the `String.map` function to write a function to return a new copy of a string with all exclamation marks replaced with periods (full stops).

5. Use the `String` module to write a function which concatenates a list of strings together.

6. Do the same with the `Buffer` module. This will be faster.

7. Use the `String` module to count the number of occurrences of the string `"OCaml"` within a given string.

So Far

1 Integers min_int ... -3 -2 -1 0 1 2 3 ... max_int of type **int**. Booleans true and false of type **bool**. Characters of type **char** like 'X' and '!'.

Mathematical operators + - * / mod which take two integers and give another.

Operators = < <= > >= <> which compare two values and evaluate to either true or false.

The conditional **if** *expression1* **then** *expression2* **else** *expression3*, where *expresssion1* has type **bool** and *expression2* and *expression3* have the same type as one another.

The boolean operators && and || which allow us to build compound boolean expressions.

2 Assigning a name to the result of evaluating an expression using the **let** *name* = *expression* construct. Building compound expressions using **let** *name1* = *expression1* **in** **let** *name2* = *expression2* **in** ...

Functions, introduced by **let** *name argument1 argument2* ... = *expression*. These have type $\alpha \rightarrow \beta$, $\alpha \rightarrow \beta \rightarrow \gamma$ etc. for some types α, β, γ etc.

Recursive functions, which are introduced in the same way, but using **let rec** instead of **let**.

3 Matching patterns using **match** *expression1* **with** *pattern1* | ... -> *expression2* | *pattern2* | ... -> *expression3* |... The expressions *expression2*, *expression3* etc. must have the same type as one another, and this is the type of the whole **match ... with** expression.

4 Lists, which are ordered collections of zero or more elements of like type. They are written between square brackets, with elements separated by semicolons e.g. [1; 2; 3; 4; 5]. If a list is non-empty, it has a head, which is its first element, and a tail, which is the list composed of the rest of the elements.

The :: "cons" operator, which adds an element to the front of a list. The @ "append" operator, which concatenates two lists together.

Lists and the :: "cons" symbol may be used for pattern matching to distinguish lists of length zero, one, etc. and with particular contents.

5 Matching two or more things at once, using commas to separate as in **match** a, b **with** 0, 0 -> *expression1* | x, y -> *expression2* | ...

6 Anonymous functions **fun** *name* -> *expression*. Making operators into functions as in (<) and (+).

7 Defining exceptions with **exception** *name*. They can carry extra information by adding **of** *type*. Raising exceptions with **raise**. Handling exceptions with **try** ... **with** ...

8 Tuples to combine a fixed number of elements (a, b), (a, b, c) etc. with types $\alpha \times \beta$, $\alpha \times \beta \times \gamma$ etc.

9 Partial application of functions by giving fewer than the full number of arguments. Partial application with functions built from operators.

10 New types with **type** *name* = *constructor1* **of** *type1* | *constructor2* **of** *type2* | ... Pattern matching on them as with the built-in types. Polymorphic types.

11 Strings, which are sequences of characters written between double quotes and are of type **string**.

12 The value () and its type **unit**. Input channels of type **in_channel** and output channels of type **out_channel**. Built-in functions for reading from and writing to them respectively.

13 References of type α **ref**. Building them using ref, accessing their contents using ! and updating them using the := operator.

Bracketing expressions together with **begin** and **end** instead of parentheses for readability.

Performing an action many times based on a boolean condition with the **while** *boolean expression* **do** *expression* **done** construct. Performing an action a fixed number of times with a varying parameter using the **for** *name* = *start* **to** *end* **do** *expression* **done** construct.

Arrays of type α **array**. Creating an array with the built-in function Array.make, finding its length with Array.length, accessing an element with a.(*subscript*). Updating with a.(*subscript*) <- *expression*. The built-in function String.iter.

14 Floating-point numbers min_float ... max_float of type **float**. Floating-point operators +. *. -. /. ** and built-in functions sqrt log etc.

15 Using functions from the OCaml Standard Library with the form *Module.function*.

Chapter 16

Building Bigger Programs

So far we have been writing little programs and testing them interactively in OCaml. However, to conquer the complexity of the task of writing larger programs, tools are needed to split them into well-defined *modules*, each with a given set of types and functions. We can then build big systems without worrying that some internal change to a single module will affect the whole program. This process of modularization is known as *abstraction*, and is fundamental to writing large programs, a discipline sometimes called *software engineering*.

In this chapter, you will have to create text files and type commands into the command prompt of your computer. If you are not sure how to do this, or the examples in this chapter do not work for you, ask a friend or teacher. In particular, if using Microsoft Windows, some of the commands may have different names.

Making a module

We will be building a modular version of our text statistics program from Chapter 13. First, write the text file shown in Figure 16.1 (but not the italic annotations) and save it as textstat.ml (OCaml programs live in files with lowercase names ending in .ml).

The first line is a comment. Comments in OCaml are written between (* and *). We use comments in

```
(* Text statistics *)                                    comment

type stats = int * int * int * int              our type for statistics

let stats_from_channel _ = (0, 0, 0, 0)         statistics from a channel

let stats_from_file filename =          and from a file; exceptions are not handled
  let channel = open_in filename in
    let result = stats_from_channel channel in
      close_in channel;
      result
```

Figure 16.1: textstat.ml

123

large programs to help the reader (who might be someone else, or ourselves some time later) to understand the program.

We have then introduced a type for our statistics. This will hold the number of words, characters, and sentences. We have then written a function `stats_from_channel` which for now just returns zeros for all the statistics.

Now, we can issue a command to turn this program into a pre-processed OCaml module. This *compiles* the program into an *executable*. The module can then be loaded into interactive OCaml, or used to build standalone programs. Execute the following command:

```
ocamlc textstate.ml
```

You can see that the name of the OCaml compiler is `ocamlc`. If there are errors in `textstat.ml` they will be printed out, including the line and character number of the problem. You must fix these, and try the command again. If compilation succeeds, you will see the file `textstate.cmo` in the current directory. There will be other files, but we are not worried about those yet. Let us load our pre-compiled module into OCaml:

```
OCaml

# #load "textstat.cmo";;                                                          load the module
# Textstat.stats_from_file "gregor.txt";;                                         use a function
- : int * int * int * int = (0, 0, 0, 0)
```

Note that `#load` is different from our earlier `#use` command – that was just reading a file as if it had been cut and pasted – we are really loading the compiled module here.

Filling out the module

Let us add a real `stats_from_channel` function, to produce a working text statistics module. We will also add utility functions for retrieving individual statistics from the `stats` type. This is shown in Figure 16.2. We can compile it in the same way, and try it with our example file:

```
OCaml

# #load "textstat.cmo";;
# let s = Textstat.stats_from_file "gregor.txt";;
val s : Textstat.stats = (8, 464, 80, 4)
# Textstat.lines s;;
- : int = 8
# Textstat.characters s;;
- : int = 464
# Textstat.words s;;
- : int = 80
# Textstat.sentences s;;
- : int = 4
```

You might ask why we need the functions `lines`, `characters` etc. when the information is returned in the tuple. Let us discuss that now.

```
(* Text statistics *)
type stats = int * int * int * int

(* Utility functions to retrieve parts of a stats value *)
let lines (l, _, _, _) = l

let characters (_, c, _, _) = c

let words (_, _, w, _) = w

let sentences (_, _, _, s) = s

(* Read statistics from a channel *)
let stats_from_channel in_channel =
  let lines = ref 0 in
  let characters = ref 0 in
  let words = ref 0 in
  let sentences = ref 0 in
    try
      while true do
        let line = input_line in_channel in
          lines := !lines + 1;
          characters := !characters + String.length line;
          String.iter
            (fun c ->
              match c with
                '.' | '?' | '!' -> sentences := !sentences + 1
              | ' ' -> words := !words + 1
              | _ -> ())
            line
      done;
      (0, 0, 0, 0) (* Just to make the type agree *)
    with
      End_of_file -> (!lines, !characters, !words, !sentences)

(* Read statistics, given a filename. Exceptions are not handled *)
let stats_from_file filename =
  let channel = open_in filename in
    let result = stats_from_channel channel in
      close_in channel;
      result
```

Figure 16.2: textstat.ml

Making an interface

We said that modules were for creating abstractions, so that the implementation of an individual module could be altered without changing the rest of the program. However, we have not achieved that yet – the details of the internal type are visible to the program using the module, and that program would break if we changed the type of `stats` to hold an additional statistic. In addition, the internal `count_words` function is available, even though the user of the module is not expected to use it.

What we would like to do is to restrict the module so that only the types and functions we want to be used directly are available. For this, we use an *interface*. Interfaces are held in files ending in `.mli`, and we can write one for our module. Our interface is shown in Figure 16.3.

In this interface, we have exposed every type and function. Types are written in the same way as in the `.ml` file. Functions are written with **val**, followed by the name, a colon, and the type of the function. We can compile this by giving the `.mli` file together with the `.ml` file when using `ocamlc`:

```
ocamlc textstat.mli textstat.ml
```

The `ocamlc` compiler has created at least two files: `textstat.cmo` as before and `textstat.cmi` (the compiled interface). You should find this operates exactly as before when loaded into OCaml. Now, let us remove the definition of the type from the interface, to make sure that the stats type is hidden, and its parts can only be accessed using the `lines`, `characters`, `words`, and `sentences` functions. We will also remove the declaration for `stats_from_channel` to demonstrate that functions we do not need can be hidden too. This is shown in Figure 16.4.

Now, if we compile the program again with `ocamlc textstat.mli textstat.ml`, we see that the `stats_of_channel` function is now not accessible, and the type of stats is now hidden, or *abstract*.

OCaml

```
# #load "textstat.cmo";;
# let s = Textstat.stats_from_file "gregor.txt";;
val s : Textstat.stats = <abstr>                          the type is now abstract
# Textstat.lines s;;
- : int = 8
# Textstat.characters s;;
- : int = 464
# Textstat.words s;;
- : int = 80
# Textstat.sentences s;;
- : int = 4
# Textstat.stats_from_channel;;                           we have hidden this function
Error: Unbound value Textstat.stats_from_channel
```

We have successfully separated the implementation of our module from its interface – we can now change the `stats` type internally to hold extra statistics without invalidating existing programs. This is abstraction in a nutshell.

```
(* Textstat module interface *)
type stats = int * int * int * int

val lines : stats -> int

val characters : stats -> int

val words : stats -> int

val sentences : stats -> int

val stats_from_channel : in_channel -> stats

val stats_from_file : string -> stats
```

Figure 16.3: textstat.mli

```
(* Textstat module interface *)
type stats

val lines : stats -> int

val characters : stats -> int

val words : stats -> int

val sentences : stats -> int

val stats_from_file : string -> stats
```

Figure 16.4: textstat.mli with hidden (abstract) type

Building standalone programs

Now it is time to cut ourselves free from interactive OCaml, and build standalone programs which can be executed directly. Let us add another file `stats.ml` which will use functions from the `Textstat` module to create a program which, when given a file name, prints some statistics about it. This is illustrated in Figure 16.5. There are some new things here:

1. The built-in array `Sys.argv` lists the arguments given to a command written at the command line. The first is the name of our program, so we ignore that. The second will be the name of the file the user wants our program to inspect. So, we match against that array. If there is any other array size, we print out a usage message.

2. The function `Printexc.to_string` from the OCaml Standard Library converts an exception into a string – we use this to print out the error.

3. There was an error, so it is convention to specify an *exit code* of 1 rather than 0. Do not worry about this.

Let us compile this standalone program using `ocamlc`, giving a name for the executable program using the `-o` option:

```
ocamlc textstat.mli textstat.ml stats.ml -o stats
```

Now, we can run the program:

```
$ ./stats gregor.txt
Words: 80
Characters: 464
Sentences: 4
Lines: 8

$ ./stats not_there.txt
An error occurred: Sys_error("not_there.txt:  No such file or directory")

$ ./stats
Usage: stats <filename>
```

This output might look different on your computer, depending on your operating system. On most computers, the `ocamlopt` compiler is also available. If we type

```
ocamlopt textstat.mli textstat.ml stats.ml -o stats
```

we obtain an executable which is much faster than before, and completely independent of OCaml – it can run on any computer which has the same processor and operating system (such as Windows or Mac OS X) as yours, with no need for an OCaml installation. On the other hand, the advantage of `ocamlc` is that it produces a program which can run on any computer, so long as OCaml support is installed.

```
(* Command line text file statistics program *)
try
  begin match Sys.argv with                              see note 1
    [|_; filename|] ->
      let stats = Textstat.stats_from_file filename in
        print_string "Words: ";
        print_int (Textstat.words stats);
        print_newline ();
        print_string "Characters: ";
        print_int (Textstat.characters stats);
        print_newline ();
        print_string "Sentences: ";
        print_int (Textstat.sentences stats);
        print_newline ();
        print_string "Lines: ";
        print_int (Textstat.lines stats);
        print_newline ()
  | _ ->
      print_string "Usage: stats <filename>";
      print_newline ()
  end
with
  e ->
    print_string "An error occurred: ";
    print_string (Printexc.to_string e);               see note 2
    print_newline ();
    exit 1                                             see note 3
```

Figure 16.5: stats.ml

Questions

1. Extend our example to print the character histogram data as we did in Chapter 13.

2. Write and compile a standalone program to reverse the lines in a text file, writing to another file.

3. Write a program which takes sufficiently long to run to allow you to compare the speed of programs compiled with `ocamlc` and `ocamlopt`.

4. Write a standalone program to search for a given string in a file. Lines where the string is found should be printed to the screen.

So Far

1 Integers `min_int` ... `-3 -2 -1 0 1 2 3` ... `max_int` of type **int**. Booleans `true` and `false` of type **bool**. Characters of type **char** like `'X'` and `'!'`.

Mathematical operators `+ - * /` `mod` which take two integers and give another.

Operators `= < <= > >= <>` which compare two values and evaluate to either `true` or `false`.

The conditional **if** *expression1* **then** *expression2* **else** *expression3*, where *expresssion1* has type **bool** and *expression2* and *expression3* have the same type as one another.

The boolean operators `&&` and `||` which allow us to build compound boolean expressions.

2 Assigning a name to the result of evaluating an expression using the **let** *name* = *expression* construct. Building compound expressions using **let** *name1* = *expression1* **in** **let** *name2* = *expression2* **in** ...

Functions, introduced by **let** *name argument1 argument2* ... = *expression*. These have type $\alpha \rightarrow \beta$, $\alpha \rightarrow \beta \rightarrow \gamma$ etc. for some types α, β, γ etc.

Recursive functions, which are introduced in the same way, but using **let rec** instead of **let**.

3 Matching patterns using **match** *expression1* **with** *pattern1* | ... -> *expression2* | *pattern2* | ... -> *expression3* | ... The expressions *expression2*, *expression3* etc. must have the same type as one another, and this is the type of the whole **match** ... **with** expression.

4 Lists, which are ordered collections of zero or more elements of like type. They are written between square brackets, with elements separated by semicolons e.g. `[1; 2; 3; 4; 5]`. If a list is non-empty, it has a head, which is its first element, and a tail, which is the list composed of the rest of the elements.

The `::` "cons" operator, which adds an element to the front of a list. The `@` "append" operator, which concatenates two lists together.

Lists and the `::` "cons" symbol may be used for pattern matching to distinguish lists of length zero, one, etc. and with particular contents.

5 Matching two or more things at once, using commas to separate as in **match** `a, b` **with** `0, 0` -> *expression1* | `x, y` -> *expression2* | ...

6 Anonymous functions **fun** *name* -> *expression*. Making operators into functions as in `( < )` and `( + )`.

7 Defining exceptions with **exception** *name*. They can carry extra information by adding **of** *type*. Raising exceptions with **raise**. Handling exceptions with **try** ... **with** ...

8 Tuples to combine a fixed number of elements `(a, b)`, `(a, b, c)` etc. with types $\alpha \times \beta$, $\alpha \times \beta \times \gamma$ etc.

9 Partial application of functions by giving fewer than the full number of arguments. Partial application with functions built from operators.

10 New types with **type** *name* = *constructor1* **of** *type1* | *constructor2* **of** *type2* | ... Pattern matching on them as with the built-in types. Polymorphic types.

11 Strings, which are sequences of characters written between double quotes and are of type **string**.

12 The value `()` and its type **unit**. Input channels of type **in_channel** and output channels of type **out_channel**. Built-in functions for reading from and writing to them respectively.

13 References of type α **ref**. Building them using `ref`, accessing their contents using `!` and updating them using the `:=` operator.

Bracketing expressions together with **begin** and **end** instead of parentheses for readability.

Performing an action many times based on a boolean condition with the **while** *boolean expression* **do** *expression* **done** construct. Performing an action a fixed number of times with a varying parameter using the **for** *name* = *start* **to** *end* **do** *expression* **done** construct.

Arrays of type α **array**. Creating an array with the built-in function `Array.make`, finding its length with `Array.length`, accessing an element with `a.(`*subscript*`)`. Updating with `a.(`*subscript*`) <-` *expression*. The built-in function `String.iter`.

14 Floating-point numbers `min_float` ... `max_float` of type **float**. Floating-point operators `+. *. -. /.` `**` and built-in functions `sqrt` `log` etc.

15 Using functions from the OCaml Standard Library with the form *Module.function*.

16 Writing modules in `.ml` files. Building interfaces in `.mli` files with types and **val**. Using the `ocamlc` and `ocamlopt` compilers. Comments written between `(*` and `*)`.

Answers to Questions

Hints may be found on page 179.

Chapter 1 (Starting Off)

1

The expression 17 is of type **int** and is a value already. The expression 1 + 2 * 3 + 4 is of type **int** and evaluates to the value 11, since the multiplication is done first. The expression 800 / 80 / 8 has type **int**. It is the same as (800 / 80) / 8 rather than 800 / (80 / 8) and evaluates to 1.

The expression 400 > 200 has type **bool** because this is the type of the result of the comparison operator >. It evaluates to true. Similarly, 1 <> 1 has type **bool** and evaluates to false. The expression true || false is of type **bool** and evaluates to true since one of the operands is true. Similarly, true && false evaluates to false since one of the operands is false. The expression **if** true **then** false **else** true evaluates to false since the first (**then**) part of the conditional expression is chosen, and takes the place of the entire expression.

The expression '%' is of type **char** and is already a value. The expression 'a' + 'b' has no type – it gives a type error because the + operator does not operate on characters.

2

The mod operator is of higher precedence than the + operator. So 1 + 2 mod 3 and 1 + (2 mod 3) are the same expression, evaluating to 1 + 2 which is 3, but (1 + 2) mod 3 is the same as 3 mod 3, which is 0.

3

The expression evaluates to 11. The programmer seems to be under the impression that spacing affects evaluation order. It does not, and so this use of space is misleading.

4

The expression max_int + 1 evaluates to a number equal to min_int. Likewise, min_int - 1 evaluates to a number equal to max_int. The number line "wraps around". This leads to the odd situation that max_int + 1 < max_int evaluates to true. It follows that when writing programs, we must be careful about what happens when numbers may be very large or very small.

5

OCaml accepts the program, but complains when it is run:

```
OCaml
```

```
# 1 / 0;;
Exception: Division_by_zero.
```

We will talk about such *exceptions* later in the book. They are used for program errors which cannot necessarily be found just by looking at the program text, but are only discovered during evaluation.

6

For x mod y:

> when $y = 0$, OCaml prints `Exception: Division_by_zero`
>
> when $y <> 0$, $x < 0$, the result will be negative
>
> when $y <> 0$, $x = 0$, the result will be zero

This illustrates how even simple mathematical operators require careful specification when programming – we must be explicit about the rules.

7

It prevents unexpected values: what would happen if an integer other than 1 and 0 was calculated in the program – what would it mean? It is better just to use a different type. We can then show more easily that a program is correct.

8

The lowercase characters are in alphabetical order, for example `'p' < 'q'` evaluates to `true`. The uppercase characters are similarly ordered. The uppercase letters are all "smaller" than the lowercase characters, so for example `'A' < 'a'` evaluates to `true`. For type **bool**, `false` is considered "less than" `true`.

Chapter 2 (Names and Functions)

1

Just take in an integer and return the number multiplied by ten. The function takes and returns an integer, so the type is **int** $\rightarrow$ **int**.

```
OCaml
```

```
# let times_ten x = x * 10;;
val times_ten : int -> int = <fun>
```

2

We must take two integer arguments, and use the && and <> operators to test if they are both non-zero. So the result will be of type **bool**. The whole type will therefore be **int** → **int** → **bool**.

OCaml

```
# let both_non_zero x y =
    x <> 0 && y <> 0;;
val both_non_zero : int -> int -> bool = <fun>
```

3

Our function should take an integer, and return another one (the sum). So, it is type will be **int** → **int**. The base case is when the number is equal to 1. Then, the sum of all numbers from $1 \ldots 1$ is just 1. If not, we add the argument to the sum of all the numbers from $1 \ldots (n-1)$.

OCaml

```
# let rec sum n =
    if n = 1 then 1 else n + sum (n - 1);;
val sum : int -> int = <fun>
```

The function is recursive, so we used **let rec** instead of **let**. What happens if the argument given is zero or negative?

4

The function will have type **int** → **int** → **int**. A number to the power of 0 is 1. A number to the power of 1 is itself. Otherwise, the answer is the current n multiplied by n^{x-1}.

OCaml

```
# let rec power x n =
    if n = 0 then 1 else
      (if n = 1 then x else
        x * power x (n - 1));;
val power : int -> int -> int = <fun>
```

Notice that we had to put one **if ... then ... else** inside the **else** part of another to cope with the three different cases. The parentheses are not actually required, though, so we may write it like this:

OCaml

```
# let rec power x n =
    if n = 0 then 1 else
      if n = 1 then x else
        x * power x (n - 1);;
val power : int -> int -> int = <fun>
```

In fact, we can remove the case for n = 1 since power x 1 will reduce to x * power x 0 which is just x.

5

The function `isconsonant` will have type **char** → **bool**. If a lower case character in the range `'a'...'z'` is not a vowel, it must be a consonant. So we can reuse the `isvowel` function we wrote earlier, and negate its result using the `not` function:

OCaml

```
# let isconsonant c = not (isvowel c);;
val isconsonant : char -> bool = <fun>
```

6

The expression is the same as **let** x = 1 **in** (**let** x = 2 **in** x + x), and so the result is 4. Both instances of x in x + x evaluate to 2 since this is the value assigned to the name x in the nearest enclosing **let** expression.

7

We could simply return 0 for a negative argument. The factorial of 0 is 1, so we can change that too, and say our new function finds the factorial of any non-negative number:

OCaml

```
# let rec factorial x =
    if x < 0 then 0 else
      if x = 0 then 1 else
        x * factorial (x - 1);;
val factorial : int -> int = <fun>
```

Note that `factorial` can fail in other ways too – if the number gets too big and "wraps around". For example, on the author's computer, `factorial 40` yields -2188836759280812032.

Chapter 3 (Case by Case)

1

We can just pattern match on the boolean. It does not matter, in this instance, which order the two cases are in.

```
not : bool → bool

let not x =
  match x with
    true -> false
  | false -> true
```

2

Recall our solution from the previous chapter:

```
sum : int → int

let rec sum n =
  if n = 1 then 1 else n + sum (n - 1)
```

Modifying it to use pattern matching:

```
sum_match : int → int

let rec sum_match n =
  match n with
    1 -> 1
  | _ -> n + sum_match (n - 1)
```

3

Again, modifying our solution from the previous chapter:

```
power_match : int → int → int

let rec power_match x n =
  match n with
    0 -> 1
  | 1 -> x
  | _ -> x * power_match x (n - 1)
```

5

This is the same as

```
match 1 + 1 with
  2 ->
    (match 2 + 2 with
      3 -> 4
    | 4 -> 5)
```

(A match case belongs to its nearest enclosing **match**). So the expression evaluates to **5**.

6

We write two functions of type **char** → **bool** like this:

```
isupper : char → bool
islower : char → bool

let isupper c =
  match c with
    'A'..'Z' -> true
  | _ -> false

let islower c =
  match c with
    'a'..'z' -> true
  | _ -> false
```

Alternatively, we might write:

```
isupper : char → bool
islower : char → bool

let isupper c =
  match c with
    'A'..'Z' -> true
  | _ -> false

let islower c =
  not (isupper c)
```

These two solutions have differing behaviour upon erroneous arguments (such as punctuation). Can you see why?

Chapter 4 (Making Lists)

1

This is similar to odd_elements:

```
even_elements : α list → α list

let rec even_elements l =
  match l with
    [] -> []                       the list has zero elements
  | [_] -> []              the list has one element – drop it
  | _::b::t -> b :: even_elements t        h is the head, t the tail
```

But we can perform the same trick as before, by reversing the cases, to reduce their number:

```
even_elements : α list → α list

let rec even_elements l =
  match l with
    _::b::t -> b :: even_elements t        drop one, keep one, carry on
  | _ -> []                                otherwise, no more to drop
```

2

This is like counting the length of a list, but we only count if the current element is true.

```
count_true : bool list → int

let rec count_true l =
  match l with
    [] -> 0                                        no more
  | true::t -> 1 + count_true t                 count this one
  | false::t -> count_true t                  but not this one
```

We can use an accumulating argument in an auxiliary function to make a tail recursive version:

```
count_true_inner : int → bool list → int
count_true : bool list → int

let rec count_true_inner n l =
  match l with
    [] -> n                        no more; return the accumulator
  | true::t -> count_true_inner (n + 1) t          count this one
  | false::t -> count_true_inner n t            but not this one

let count_true l =
  count_true_inner 0 l               initialize the accumulator with zero
```

3

To make a palindrome from any list, we can append it to its reverse. To check if a list is a palindrome, we can compare it for equality with its reverse (the comparison operators work over almost all types).

```
mk_palindrome : α list → α list
is_palindrome : α list → bool

let mk_palindrome l =
  l @ rev l

let is_palindrome l =
  l = rev l
```

4

We pattern match with three cases. The empty list, where we have reached the last element, and where we have yet to reach it.

```
drop_last : α list → α list

let rec drop_last l =
  match l with
    [] -> []
  | [_] -> []            it is the last one, so remove it
  | h::t -> h :: drop_last t      at least two elements remain
```

We can build a tail recursive version by adding an accumulating list, and reversing it when finished (assuming a tail recursive rev, of course!)

```
drop_last_inner : α list → α list → α list
drop_last : α list → α list

let rec drop_last_inner a l =
  match l with
    [] -> rev a              return the reversed accumulator
  | [_] -> rev a             same, ignoring the last element
  | h::t -> drop_last_inner (h :: a) t    at least two elements remain

let drop_last l =
  drop_last_inner [] l
```

5

The empty list cannot contain the element; if there is a non-empty list, either the head is equal to the element we are looking for, or if not, the result of our function is just the same as the result of recursing on the tail.

Note that we are using the property that the || operator only evaluates its right hand side if the left hand side is false to limit the recursion – it really does stop as soon as it finds the element.

```
member : α → α list → bool

let rec member e l =
  match l with
    [] -> false
  | h::t -> h = e || member e t
```

6

If a list is empty, it is already a set. If not, either the head exists somewhere in the tail or it does not; if it does exist in the tail, we can discard it, since it will be included later. If not, we must include it.

```
make_set : α list → α list

let rec make_set l =
  match l with
    [] -> []
  | h::t -> if member h t then make_set t else h :: make_set t
```

For example, consider the evaluation of make_set [4; 5; 6; 5; 4]:

$$
\begin{aligned}
&\text{make\_set } [4;\ 5;\ 6;\ 5;\ 4] \\
\implies &\text{make\_set } [5;\ 6;\ 5;\ 4] \\
\implies &\text{make\_set } [6;\ 5;\ 4] \\
\implies &6 :: \text{make\_set } [5;\ 4] \\
\implies &6 :: 5 :: \text{make\_set } [4] \\
\implies &6 :: 5 :: 4 :: \text{make\_set } [] \\
\implies &6 :: 5 :: 4 :: [] \\
\overset{*}{\implies} &[6;\ 5;\ 4]
\end{aligned}
$$

7

The first part of the evaluation of rev takes time proportional to the length of the list, processing each element once. However, when the lists are appended together, the order of the operations is such that the first argument becomes longer each time. The @ operator, as we know, also takes time proportional to the length of its first argument. And so, this accumulating of the lists takes time proportional to the square of the length of the list.

$$
\begin{array}{ll}
& \texttt{rev [1; 2; 3; 4]} \\
\Longrightarrow & \texttt{rev [2; 3; 4] @ [1]} \\
\Longrightarrow & \texttt{(rev [3; 4] @ [2]) @ [1]} \\
\Longrightarrow & \texttt{((rev [4] @ [3]) @ [2]) @ [1]} \\
\Longrightarrow & \texttt{(((rev [] @ [4]) @ [3]) @ [2]) @ [1]} \\
\Longrightarrow & \texttt{(((([] @ [4]) @ [3]) @ [2]) @ [1]} \\
\Longrightarrow & \texttt{(([4] @ [3]) @ [2]) @ [1]} \\
\Longrightarrow & \texttt{([4; 3] @ [2]) @ [1]} \\
\Longrightarrow & \texttt{[4; 3; 2] @ [1]} \\
\Longrightarrow & \texttt{[4; 3; 2; 1]}
\end{array}
$$

By using an additional accumulating argument, we can write a version which operates in time proportional to the length of the list.

```
rev_inner : α list → α list → α list
rev : α list → α list

let rec rev_inner a l =
  match l with
    [] -> a
  | h::t -> rev_inner (h :: a) t

let rev l =
  rev_inner [] l
```

For the same list:

$$
\begin{array}{ll}
& \texttt{rev [1; 2; 3; 4]} \\
\Longrightarrow & \texttt{rev\_inner [] [1; 2; 3; 4]} \\
\Longrightarrow & \texttt{rev\_inner [1] [2; 3; 4]} \\
\Longrightarrow & \texttt{rev\_inner [2; 1] [3; 4]} \\
\Longrightarrow & \texttt{rev\_inner [3; 2; 1] [4]} \\
\Longrightarrow & \texttt{rev\_inner [4; 3; 2; 1] []} \\
\Longrightarrow & \texttt{[4; 3; 2; 1]}
\end{array}
$$

Chapter 5 (Sorting Things)

1

Simply add an extra **let** to define a name representing the number we will take or drop:

```
msort : α list → α list

let rec msort l =
  match l with
    [] -> []                              we are done if the list is empty
  | [x] -> [x]                       and also if it only has one element
  | _ ->
      let x = length l / 2 in
        let left = take x l in                      get the left hand half
          let right = drop x l in                  and the right hand half
            merge (msort left) (msort right)           sort and merge them
```

2

The argument to `take` or `drop` is `length l / 2` which is clearly less than or equal to `length l` for all possible values of `l`. Thus, `take` and `drop` always succeed. In our case, `take` and `drop` are only called with `length l` is more than 1, due to the pattern matching.

3

We may simply replace the <= operator with the >= operator in the `insert` function.

```
insert : α → α list → α list

let rec insert x l =
  match l with
    [] -> [x]
  | h::t ->
      if x >= h
        then x :: h :: t
        else h :: insert x t
```

The `sort` function is unaltered.

4

We require a function of type α **list** → **bool**. List of length zero and one are, by definition, sorted. If the list is longer, check that its first two elements are in sorted order. If this is true, also check that the rest of the list is sorted, starting with the second element.

```
is_sorted : α list → bool

let rec is_sorted l =
  match l with
    [] -> true
  | [x] -> true
  | a::b::t -> a <= b && is_sorted (b :: t)
```

We can reverse the cases to simplify:

```
is_sorted : α list → bool

let rec is_sorted l =
  match l with
    a::b::t -> a <= b && is_sorted (b :: t)
  | _ -> true
```

5

Lists are compared starting with their first elements. If the elements differ, they are compared, and that is the result of the comparison. If both have the same first element, the second elements are considered, and so on. If the end of one list is reached before the other, the shorter list is considered smaller. For example:

[1] < [2] < [2; 1] < [2; 2]

These are the same principles you use to look up a word in a dictionary: compare the first letters – if same, compare the second etc. So, when applied to the example in the question, it has the effect of sorting the words into alphabetical order.

6

The **let rec** construct can be nested just like the **let** construct:

```
sort : α list → α list

let rec sort l =
  let rec insert x s =
    match s with
      [] -> [x]
    | h::t ->
        if x <= h
          then x :: h :: t
          else h :: insert x t
  in
    match l with
      [] -> []
    | h::t -> insert h (sort t)
```

We have renamed the second argument of the insert function to avoid confusion.

Chapter 6 (Functions upon Functions upon Functions)

1

Our function will have type **char list** → **char list**. We just match on the argument list: if it is empty, we are done. If it starts with an exclamation mark, we output a period, and carry on. If not, we output the character unchanged, and carry on:

```
calm : char list → char list

let rec calm l =
  match l with
    [] -> []
  | '!'::t -> '.' :: calm t
  | h::t -> h :: calm t
```

To use map instead, we write a simple function `calm_char` to process a single character. We can then use map to build our main function:

```
calm_char : char → char
calm : char list → char list

let calm_char x =
  match x with '!' -> '.' | _ -> x

let calm l =
  map calm_char l
```

This avoids the explicit recursion of the original, and so it is easier to see what is going on.

2

The `clip` function is of type **int** → **int** and is easy to write:

```
clip : int → int

let clip x =
  if x < 1 then 1 else
    if x > 10 then 10 else x
```

Now we can use map for the `cliplist` function:

```
cliplist : int list → int list

let cliplist l =
  map clip l
```

3

Just put the body of the clip function inside an anonymous function:

```
cliplist : int list → int list

let cliplist l =
  map
    (fun x ->
       if x < 1 then 1 else
         if x > 10 then 10 else x)
    l
```

4

We require a function apply f n x which applies function f a total of n times to the initial value x. The base case is when n is zero.

```
apply : (α → α) → int → α → α

let rec apply f n x =
  if n = 0
    then x                                                    just x
    else f (apply f (n - 1) x)              reduce problem size by one
```

Consider the type:

$$\underbrace{(\alpha \to \alpha)}_{\text{function f}} \to \underbrace{\mathbf{int}}_{n} \to \underbrace{\alpha}_{x} \to \underbrace{\alpha}_{\text{result}}$$

The function f must take and return the same type α, since its result in one iteration is fed back in as its argument in the next. Therefore, the argument x and the final result must also have type α. For example, for $\alpha = \mathbf{int}$, we might have a power function:

```
power : int → int → int

let power a b =
  apply (fun x -> x * a) b 1
```

So power a b calculates a^b.

5

We can add an extra argument to the insert function, and use that instead of the comparison operator:

```
insert : (α → α → bool) → α → α list → α list

let rec insert f x l =                          add extra argument f
  match l with
    [] -> [x]
  | h::t ->
      if f x h
        then x :: h :: t
        else h :: insert f x t          remember to add f here too
```

Now we just need to rewrite the sort function.

```
sort : (α → α → bool) → α list → α list

let rec sort f l =
  match l with
    [] -> []
  | h::t -> insert f h (sort f t)
```

6

We cannot use map here, because the result list will not necessarily be the same length as the argument list. The function will have type $(\alpha \to \textbf{bool}) \to \alpha$ **list** $\to \alpha$ **list**.

```
filter : (α → bool) → α list → α list

let rec filter f l =
  match l with
    [] -> []
  | h::t ->
      if f h
        then h :: filter f t
        else filter f t
```

For example, filter (**fun** x -> x mod 2 = 0) [1; 2; 4; 5] evaluates to [2; 4].

7

The function will have type $(\alpha \to \textbf{bool}) \to \alpha$ **list** $\to$ **bool**.

```
for_all : (α → bool) → α list → bool

let rec for_all f l =
  match l with
    [] -> true
  | h::t -> f h && for_all f t          true for this one, and all the others
```

For example, we can see if all elements of a list are positive: `for_all (fun x -> x > 0) [1; 2; -1]` evaluates to `false`. Notice that we are relying on the fact that && only evaluates its right hand side when the left hand side is true to limit the recursion.

8

The function will have type $(α → β) → α$ **list list** $→ β$ **list list**. We use map on each element of the list.

```
mapl : (α → β) → α list list → β list list

let rec mapl f l =
  match l with
    [] -> []
  | h::t -> map f h :: mapl f t
```

We have used explicit recursion to handle the outer list, and map to handle each inner list.

Chapter 7 (When Things Go Wrong)

1

The function `smallest_inner` takes a currently smallest found integer, a boolean value `found` indicating if we have found any suitable value or not, and the list of integers. It is started with `max_int` as the current value, so that any number is smaller than it, and `false` for `found` because nothing has been found yet.

```
smallest_inner : int → bool → int list → int
smallest : int list → int

let rec smallest_inner current found l =
  match l with
    [] ->
      if found then current else raise Not_found
  | h::t ->
      if h > 0 && h < current
        then smallest_inner h true t
        else smallest_inner current found t

let smallest l =
  smallest_inner max_int false l
```

Thus, the function raises an exception in the case of an empty list, or one which is non-empty but contains no positive integer, and otherwise returns the smallest positive integer in the list.

2

We just surround the call to smallest with an exception handler for Not_found.

```
smallest_or_zero : int list → int

let smallest_or_zero l =
  try smallest l with Not_found -> 0
```

3

We write a function sqrt_inner which, given a test number x and a target number n squares x and tests if it is more than n. If it is, the answer is x - 1. The test number will be initialized at 1. The function sqrt raises our exception if the argument is less than zero, and otherwise begins the testing process.

```
sqrt_inner : int → int → int
sqrt : int → int

let rec sqrt_inner x n =
  if x * x > n then x - 1 else sqrt_inner (x + 1) n

exception Complex

let sqrt n =
  if n < 0 then raise Complex else sqrt_inner 1 n
```

4

We wrap up the function, handle the Complex exception and return.

```
safe_sqrt : int → int

let safe_sqrt n =
  try sqrt n with Complex -> 0
```

Chapter 8 (Looking Things Up)

1

Since the keys must be unique, the number of different keys is simply the length of the list representing the dictionary – so we can just use the usual length function.

2

The type is the same as for the **add** function. However, if we reach the end of the list, we raise an exception, since we did not manage to find the entry to replace.

```
replace : α → β → (α × β) list → (α × β) list

let rec replace k v l =
  match l with
    [] -> raise Not_found                              could not find it; fail
  | (k', v')::t ->
      if k = k'
        then (k, v) :: t                               found it – replace
        else (k', v') :: replace k v t                 keep it, and keep looking
```

3

The function takes a list of keys and a list of values and returns a dictionary. So it will have type α **list** $\rightarrow$ β **list** $\rightarrow$ $(\alpha \times \beta)$ **list**.

```
mkdict : α list → β list → (α × β) list

let rec mkdict keys values =
  match keys, values with
    [], [] -> []
  | [], _ -> raise (Invalid_argument "mkdict")         unequal length
  | _, [] -> raise (Invalid_argument "mkdict")          ditto
  | k::ks, v::vs -> (k, v) :: mkdict ks vs      make one pair, and move on
```

4

This will have the type $(\alpha \times \beta)$ **list** $\rightarrow$ α **list** $\times$ β **list**. For the first time, we need to return a pair, building up both result lists element by element. This is rather awkward, since we will need the tails of both of the eventual results, so we can attach the new heads. We can do this by pattern matching.

```
mklists : (α × β) list → α list × β list

let rec mklists l =
  match l with
    [] -> ([], [])                                     build the empty pair
  | (k, v)::more ->                          we have at least one key-value pair
      match mklists more with                          make the rest
        (ks, vs) -> (k :: ks, v :: vs)                 and attach k and v
```

Here's a sample evaluation (we cannot really show it in the conventional way, so you must work through it whilst looking at the function definition):

$$
\begin{array}{rl}
& \texttt{mklists [(1, 2); (3, 4); (5, 6)]} \\
\implies & \texttt{mklists [(3, 4); (5, 6)]} \\
\implies & \texttt{mklists [(5, 6)]} \\
\implies & \texttt{mklists []} \\
\implies & \texttt{([], [])} \\
\implies & \texttt{([5], [6])} \\
\implies & \texttt{([3; 5], [4; 6])} \\
\implies & \texttt{([1; 3; 5], [2; 4; 6])}
\end{array}
$$

Since the inner pattern match has only one form, and is complete, we can use **let** instead:

```
mklists : (α × β) list → α list × β list

let rec mklists l =
  match l with
    [] -> ([], [])                                    build the empty pair
  | (k, v)::more ->                     we have at least one key-value pair
      let (ks, vs) = mklists more in                         make the rest
        (k :: ks, v :: vs)                             and attach k and v
```

5

We can use our `member` function which determines whether an element is a member of a list, building up a list of the keys we have already seen, and adding to the result list of key-value pairs only those with new keys.

```
dictionary_of_pairs_inner : α list → (α × β) list → (α × β) list
dictionary_of_pairs : (α × β) list → (α × β) list

let rec dictionary_of_pairs_inner keys_seen l =
  match l with
    [] -> []
  | (k, v)::t ->
      if member k keys_seen
        then dictionary_of_pairs_inner keys_seen t
        else (k, v) :: dictionary_of_pairs_inner (k :: keys_seen) t

let dictionary_of_pairs l =
  dictionary_of_pairs_inner [] l
```

How long does this take to run? Consider how long `member` takes.

6

We pattern match on the first list – if it is empty, the result is simply b. Otherwise, we add the first element of the first list to the union of the rest of its elements and the second list.

```
union : (α × β) list → (α × β) list → (α × β) list

let rec union a b =
  match a with
    [] -> b
  | (k, v)::t -> add k v (union t b)
```

We can verify that the elements of dictionary a have precedence over the elements of dictionary b by noting that add replaces a value if the key already exists.

Chapter 9 (More with Functions)

1

The function g a b c has type $\alpha \to \beta \to \gamma \to \delta$ which can also be written $\alpha \to (\beta \to (\gamma \to \delta))$. Thus, it takes an argument of type α and returns a function of type $\beta \to (\gamma \to \delta)$ which, when you give it an argument of type β returns a function of type $\gamma \to \delta$ which, when you give it an argument of type γ returns something of type δ. And so, we can apply just one or two arguments to the function g (which is called partial application), or apply all three at once. When we write **let** g a b c = ... this is just shorthand for **let** g = **fun** a -> **fun** b -> **fun** c -> ...

2

The type of member is $\alpha \to \alpha$ **list** $\to$ **bool**, so if we partially apply the first argument, the type of member x must be α **list** $\to$ **bool**. We can use the partially-applied member function and map to produce a list of boolean values, one for each list in the argument, indicating whether or not that list contains the element. Then, we can use member again to make sure there are no false booleans in the list.

```
member_all : α → α list list → bool

let member_all x ls =
  let booleans = map (member x) ls in
    not (member false booleans)
```

We could also write:

```
member_all : α → α list list → bool

let member_all x ls =
  not (member false (map (member x) ls))
```

Which do you think is clearer? Why do we check for the absence of `false` rather than the presence of `true`?

3

The function (/) 2 resulting from the partial application of the / operator is the function which divides two by a given number, not the function which divides a given number by two. We can define a reverse divide function...

```
let rdiv x y = y / x
```

... which, when partially applied, does what we want.

4

The function map has type $(\alpha \rightarrow \beta) \rightarrow \alpha$ **list** $\rightarrow \beta$ **list**. The function `mapl` we wrote has type $(\alpha \rightarrow \beta) \rightarrow \alpha$ **list list** $\rightarrow \beta$ **list list**. So the function `mapll` will have type $(\alpha \rightarrow \beta) \rightarrow \alpha$ **list list list** $\rightarrow \beta$ **list list list**. It may be defined thus:

```
mapll : (α → β) → α list list list → β list list list

let mapll f l = map (map (map f)) l
```

But, as discussed, we may remove the `l`s too:

```
mapll : (α → β) → α list list list → β list list list

let mapll f = map (map (map f))
```

It is not possible to write a function which would map a function f over a list, or list of lists, or list of lists of lists depending upon its argument, because every function in OCaml must have a single type. If a function could map f over an α **list list** it must inspect its argument enough to know it is a list of lists, thus it could not be used on a β **list** unless $\beta = \alpha$ **list**.

5

We can write a function to truncate a single list using our `take` function, being careful to deal with the case where there is not enough to take, and then use this and `map` to build `truncate` itself.

```
truncate_l : int → α list → α list
truncate : int → α list list → α list list

let truncate_l n l =
  if length l >= n then take n l else l

let truncate n ll =
  map (truncate_l n) ll
```

Here we have used partial application of `truncate` to build a suitable function for `map`. Note that we could use exception handling instead of calling length, saving time:

```
truncate_l : int → α list → α list
truncate : int → α list list → α list list

let truncate_l n l =
  try take n l with Invalid_argument "take" -> l

let truncate n ll =
  map (truncate_l n) ll
```

You might, however, reflect on whether or not this is good style.

6

First, define a function which takes the given number and a list, returning the first element (or the number if none). We can then build the main function, using partial application to make a suitable function to give to `map`:

```
firstelt : α → α list → α
firstelts : α → α list list → α list

let firstelt n l =
  match l with [] -> n | h::_ -> h

let firstelts n l =
  map (firstelt n) l
```

Chapter 10 (New Kinds of Data)

1

We need two constructors – one for squares, which needs just a single integer (the length of a side), and one for rectangles which needs two integers (the width and height, in that order):

```
type rect =
  Square of int
| Rectangle of int * int
```

The name of our new type is rect. A rect is either a `Square` or a `Rectangle`. For example,

```
s : rect
r : rect

let s = Square 7

let r = Rectangle (5, 2)                                    width 5, height 2
```

2

We pattern match on the argument:

```
area : rect → int

let area r =
  match r with
    Square s -> s * s
  | Rectangle (w, h) -> w * h
```

3

This will be a function of type rect → rect. Squares remain unaltered, but if we have a rectangle with a
bigger width than height, we rotate it by ninety degrees.

```
rotate : rect → rect

let rect r =
  match r with
    Rectangle (w, h) ->
      if w > h then Rectangle (h, w) else r
  | Square _ -> r
```

4

We will use map to perform our rotation on any rects in the argument list which need it. We will then use
the sorting function from the previous chapter which takes a custom comparison function so as to just
compare the widths.

```
width_of_rect : rect → int
rect_compare : rect → rect → bool
pack : rect list → rect list

let width_of_rect r =
  match r with
    Square s -> s
  | Rectangle (w, _) -> w

let rect_compare a b =
  width_of_rect a < width_of_rect b

let pack rects =
  sort rect_compare (map rotate rects)
```

For example, packing the list of rects

```
    [Square 6; Rectangle (4, 3); Rectangle (5, 6); Square 2]
```

will give

```
    [Square 2; Rectangle (3, 4); Rectangle (5, 6); Square 6]
```

5

We follow the same pattern as for the **list** type, being careful to deal with exceptional circumstances:

```
take : int → α sequence → α sequence
drop : int → α sequence → α sequence
map : (α → β) → α sequence → β sequence

let rec take n l =
  if n = 0 then Nil else
    match l with
      Nil -> raise (Invalid_argument "take")
    | Cons (h, t) -> Cons (h, take (n - 1) t)

let rec drop n l =
  if n = 0 then l else
    match l with
      Nil -> raise (Invalid_argument "drop")
    | Cons (_, l) -> drop (n - 1) l

let rec map f l =
  match l with
    Nil -> Nil
  | Cons (h, t) -> Cons (f h, map f t)
```

6

We can use our `power` function from earlier:

```
type expr =
  Num of int
| Add of expr * expr
| Subtract of expr * expr
| Multiply of expr * expr
| Divide of expr * expr
| Power of expr * expr

evaluate : expr → int

let rec evaluate e =
  match e with
    Num x -> x
  | Add (e, e') -> evaluate e + evaluate e'
  | Subtract (e, e') -> evaluate e - evaluate e'
  | Multiply (e, e') -> evaluate e * evaluate e'
  | Divide (e, e') -> evaluate e / evaluate e'
  | Power (e, e') -> power (evaluate e) (evaluate e')
```

7

We can just wrap up the previous function:

```
evaluate_opt : expr → int option

let evaluate_opt e =
  try Some (evaluate e) with Division_by_zero -> None
```

Chapter 11 (Growing Trees)

1

Our function will have type $\alpha \to \alpha$ tree $\to$ **bool**. It takes a element to look for, a tree holding that kind of element, and returns `true` if the element is found, or `false` otherwise.

```
member_tree : α → α tree → bool

let rec member_tree x tr =
  match tr with
    Lf -> false
  | Br (y, l, r) -> x = y || member_tree x l || member_tree x r
```

Note that we have placed the test x = y first of the three to ensure earliest termination upon finding an appropriate element.

2

Our function will have type α tree $\rightarrow$ α tree. A leaf flips to a leaf. A branch has its left and right swapped, and we must recursively flip its left and right sub-trees too.

```
flip_tree : α tree → α tree

let rec flip_tree tr =
  match tr with
    Lf -> Lf
  | Br (x, l, r) -> Br (x, flip_tree r, flip_tree l)
```

3

We can check each part of both trees together. Leaves are considered equal, branches are equal if their left and right sub-trees are equal.

```
equal_shape : α tree → β tree → bool

let rec equal_shape tr tr2 =
  match tr, tr2 with
    Lf, Lf ->
      true
  | Br (_, l, r), Br (_, l2, r2) ->
      equal_shape l l2 && equal_shape r r2
  | _, _ ->
      false
```

4

We can use the tree insertion operation repeatedly:

```
tree_of_list : (α × β) list → (α × β) tree

let rec tree_of_list l =
  match l with
    [] -> Lf
  | (k, v)::t -> insert (tree_of_list t) k v
```

There will be no key clashes, because the argument should already be a dictionary. If it is not, earlier keys are preferred since insert replaces existing keys.

5

We can make list dictionaries from both tree dictionaries, append them, and build a new tree from the resultant list.

```
tree_union : (α × β) tree → (α × β) tree → (α × β) tree

let tree_union t t' =
  tree_of_list (list_of_tree t @ list_of_tree t')
```

The combined list may not be a dictionary (because it may have repeated keys), but `tree_of_list` will prefer keys encountered earlier. So, we put entries from `t'` after those from `t`.

6

We will use a list for the sub-trees of each branch, with the empty list signifying there are no more i.e. that this is the bottom of the tree. Thus, we only need a single constructor.

```
type 'a mtree = Branch of 'a * 'a mtree list
```

So, now we can define `size`, `total`, and `map`.

```
size : α mtree → int
total : α mtree → int
map_mtree : (α → β) → α mtree → β mtree

let rec size tr =
  match tr with
    Branch (e, l) -> 1 + sum (map size l)

let rec total tr =
  match tr with
    Branch (e, l) -> e + sum (map total l)

let rec map_mtree f tr =
  match tr with
    Branch (e, l) -> Branch (f e, map (map_mtree f) l)
```

In fact, when there is only one pattern to match, we can put it directly in place of the function's argument, simplifying these definitions:

```
size  :  α mtree → int
total  :  α mtree → int
map_mtree  :  (α → β) → α mtree → β mtree

let rec size (Branch (e, l)) =
  1 + sum (map size l)

let rec total (Branch (e, l)) =
  e + sum (map total l)

let rec map_mtree f (Branch (e, l)) =
  Branch (f e, map (map_mtree f) l)
```

Chapter 12 (In and Out)

1

A first attempt might be:

```
print_integers  :  int list → unit

let print_integers l =
  print_string "[";
  iter (fun i -> print_int i; print_string "; ") l;
  print_string "]"
```

However, there are two problems:

```
        OCaml
```

```
# [1; 2; 3];;
- : int list = [1; 2; 3]
# print_integers [1; 2; 3];;
[1; 2; 3; ]- : unit = ()
```

There is an extra space after the last element, and a semicolon too. We can fix this, at the cost of a longer program:

```
print_integers_inner : int list → unit
print_integers : int list → unit

let rec print_integers_inner l =
  match l with
    [] -> ()
  | [i] -> print_int i
  | h::t -> print_int h; print_string "; "; print_integers_inner t

let print_integers l =
  print_string "[";
  print_integers_inner l;
  print_string "]"
```

Now, the result is correct:

```
                    OCaml

# [1; 2; 3];;
- : int list = [1; 2; 3]
# print_integers [1; 2; 3];;
[1; 2; 3]- : unit = ()
```

2

We must deal with the exception raised when read_int attempts to read something which is not an integer, as before. When that exception is caught, we try again, by recursively calling ourselves. The function ends when three integers are input correctly, returning them as a tuple.

```
read_three : unit → int × int × int

let rec read_three () =
  try
    print_string "Type three integers, pressing Enter after each";
    print_newline ();
    let x = read_int () in
      let y = read_int () in
        let z = read_int () in
          (x, y, z)
  with
    Failure "int_of_string" ->
      print_string "Failed to read integers; please try again";
      print_newline ();
      read_three ()
```

You may wonder why we used nested **let ... in** structures rather than just writing (read_int (), read_int (), read_int ()) – the evaluation order of a tuple is not specified and OCaml is free to do what it wants.

3

We ask the user how many dictionary entries will be entered, eliminating the need for a special "I have finished" code. First, a function to read a given number of integer–string pairs, dealing with the usual problem of malformed integers:

```
read_dict_number : int → (int × string) list

let rec read_dict_number n =
  if n = 0 then [] else
    try
      let i = read_int () in
        let name = read_line () in
          (i, name) :: read_dict_number (n - 1)
    with
      Failure "int_of_string" ->
        print_string "This is not a valid integer.";
        print_newline ();
        print_string "Please enter integer and name again.";
        print_newline ();
        read_dict_number n
```

And now, asking the user how many entries there will be, and calling our first function:

```
read_dict : unit → (int × string) list

exception BadNumber

let rec read_dict () =
  print_string "How many dictionary entries to input?";
  print_newline ();
  try
    let n = read_int () in
      if n < 0 then raise BadNumber else read_dict_number n
  with
    Failure "int_of_string" ->
      print_string "Not a number. Try again";
      print_newline ();
      read_dict ()
  | BadNumber ->
      print_string "Number is negative. Try again";
      print_newline ();
      read_dict ()
```

Notice that we defined, raised, and handled our own exception BadNumber to deal with the user asking to read a negative number of dictionary entries – this would cause read_dict_number to fail to return.

4

If we write a function to build the list of integers from 1 to n (or the empty list if n is zero):

```
numlist : int → int list

let rec numlist n =
  match n with
    0 -> []
  | _ -> numlist (n - 1) @ [n]
```

We can then write a function to output a table of a given size to an output channel.

```
write_table_channel : in_channel → int → unit

let write_table_channel ch n =
  iter
    (fun x ->
       iter
         (fun i ->
           output_string ch (string_of_int i);
           output_string ch "\t")
         (map (( * ) x) (numlist n));
       output_string ch "\n")
    (numlist n)
```

Look at this carefully. We are using nested calls to iter to build the two-dimensional table from one-dimensional lists. Can you separate this into more than one function? Which approach do you think is more readable?

We can test write_table_channel most easily by using the built-in output channel stdout which just writes to the screen:

```
OCaml
```

```
# write_table_channel stdout 5;;
1       2       3       4       5
2       4       6       8       10
3       6       9       12      15
4       8       12      16      20
5       10      15      20      25
- : unit = ()
```

Now we just need to wrap it in a function to open an output file, write the table, and close the output, dealing with any errors which may arise.

```
table : string → int → unit

exception FileProblem

let table filename n =
  if n < 0 then raise (Invalid_argument "table") else
    try
      let ch = open_out filename in
        write_table_channel ch n;
        close_out ch
    with
      _ -> raise FileProblem
```

In addition to raising `Invalid_argument` in the case of a negative number, we handle all possible exceptions to do with opening, writing to, and closing the file, re-raising them as our own, predefined one. Is this good style?

5

We write a simple function to count the lines in a channel by taking a line, ignoring it, and adding one to the result of taking another line; our recursion ends when an `End_of_file` exception is raised – it is caught and 0 ends the summation.

The main function `countlines` just opens the file, calls the first function, and closes the file. Any errors are caught and re-raised using the built-in `Failure` exception.

```
countlines_channel : in_channel → int
countlines : string → int

let rec countlines_channel ch =
  try
    let _ = input_line ch in
      1 + countlines_channel ch
  with
    End_of_file -> 0

let countlines file =
  try
    let ch = open_in file in
      let result = countlines_channel ch in
        close_in ch;
        result
  with
    _ -> raise (Failure "countlines")
```

6

As usual, let us write a function to deal with channels, and then deal with opening and closing files afterward. Our function takes an input channel and an output channel, adds the line read from the input to the output, follows it with a newline character, and continues. It only ends when the End_of_file exception is raised inside input_line and caught.

```
copy_file_ch : in_channel → out_channel → unit

let rec copy_file_ch from_ch to_ch =
  try
    output_string to_ch (input_line from_ch);
    output_string to_ch "\n";
    copy_file_ch from_ch to_ch
  with
    End_of_file -> ()
```

Now we wrap it up, remembering to open and close both files and deal with the many different errors which might occur.

```
copy_file : string → string → unit

exception CopyFailed

let copy_file from_name to_name =
  try
    let from_ch = open_in from_name in
      let to_ch = open_out to_name in
        copy_file_ch from_ch to_ch;
        close_in from_ch;
        close_out to_ch
  with
    _ -> raise CopyFailed
```

Chapter 13 (Putting Things in Boxes)

1

Two references, x and y, of type **int ref** have been created. Their initial values are 1 and 2. Their final values are 2 and 4. The type of the expression is **int** because this is the type of !x + !y, and the result is 6.

2

The expression [ref 5; ref 5] is of type **int ref list**. It contains two references each containing the integer 5. Changing the contents of one reference will not change the contents of the other. The expression **let** x = ref 5 **in** [x; x] is also of type **int ref list** and also contains two references to the integer 5. However, altering one will alter the other:

    OCaml

```
# let r = let x = ref 5 in [x; x];;
val r : int ref list = [{contents = 5}; {contents = 5}]
# match r with h::_ -> h := 6;;
Warning 8: this pattern-matching is not exhaustive.
Here is an example of a value that is not matched:
[]
- : unit = ()
# r;;
- : int ref list = [{contents = 6}; {contents = 6}]
```

3

We can write a function `forloop` which takes a function of type **int** $\rightarrow \alpha$ (where alpha would normally be **unit**), together with the start and end numbers:

```
forloop : (int → α) → int → int → unit

let rec forloop f n m =
  if n <= m then
    begin
      f n;
      forloop f (n + 1) m
    end
```

For example:

        OCaml

```
# forloop print_int 2 10;;
2345678910- : unit = ()
# forloop print_int 2 2;;
2- : unit = ()
```

4

[|1; 2; 3|] : **int array**

[|true; false; true|] : **bool array**

[|[|1|]|] : (**int array**) **array** which is **int array array**

[|[1; 2; 3]; [4; 5; 6]|] : **int list array**

[|1; 2; 3|].(2) : **int**, has value 2

[|1; 2; 3|].(2) <- 4 : **unit**, updates the array to [|1; 2; 4|]

5

We use a **for** construct:

```
array_sum : int array → int

let array_sum a =
  let sum = ref 0 in
    for x = 0 to Array.length a - 1 do
      sum := !sum + a.(x)
    done;
    !sum
```

Note that this works for the empty array, because a **for** construct where the second number is less than the first never executes its expression.

6

Since we wish to reverse the array in place, our function will have type α **array** $\rightarrow$ **unit**. Our method is to proceed from the first element to the half-way point, swapping elements from either end of the array. If the array has odd length, the middle element will not be altered.

```
array_rev : α array → unit

let array_rev a =
  if a <> [||] then
    for x = 0 to Array.length a / 2 do
      let t = a.(x) in
        a.(x) <- a.(Array.length a - 1 - x);
        a.(Array.length a - 1 - x) <- t
    done
```

Note that we must check for the case where the array is empty; otherwise there would be an invalid attempt to access element zero inside the **for** loop.

7

We will represent the **int array array** as an array of columns so that a.(x).(y) is the element in column x and row y.

```
table : int → int array array

let table n =
  let a = Array.make n [||] in
    for x = 0 to n - 1 do
      a.(x) <- Array.make n 0
    done;
    for y = 0 to n - 1 do
      for x = 0 to n - 1 do
        a.(x).(y) <- (x + 1) * (y + 1)
      done
    done;
    a
```

Note that the result is correct for `table 0`.

8

The difference between the codes for `'a'` and `'A'`, or `'z'` and `'Z'` is 32, so we add or subtract as appropriate. Codes not in those ranges are unaltered.

```
uppercase : char → char
lowercase : char → char

let uppercase x =
  if int_of_char x >= 97 && int_of_char x <= 122
    then char_of_int (int_of_char x - 32)
    else x

let lowercase x =
  if int_of_char x >= 65 && int_of_char x <= 90
    then char_of_int (int_of_char x + 32)
    else x
```

9

Periods, exclamation marks and question marks may appear in multiples, leading to a wrong answer. The number of characters does not include newlines. It is not clear how quotations would be handled. Counting the words by counting spaces is inaccurate – a line with ten words will count only nine.

Chapter 14 (The Other Numbers)

1

We calculate the ceiling and floor, and return the closer one, being careful to make sure that a point equally far from the ceiling and floor is rounded up.

```
round : float → float

let round x =
  let c = ceil x in
    let f = floor x in
      if c -. x <= x -. f then c else f
```

The behaviour with regard to values such as `infinity` and `nan` is fine, since it always returns the result of either `floor` or `ceil`.

2

The function returns another point, and is simple arithmetic.

```
between : float × float → float × float → float × float

let between (x, y) (x', y') =
  ((x +. x') /. 2., (y +. y') /. 2.)
```

3

The whole part is calculated using the built-in `floor` function. We return a tuple, the first number being the whole part, the second being the original number minus the whole part. In the case of a negative number, we must be careful – `floor` always rounds downward, not toward zero!

```
parts : float → float × float

let rec parts x =
  if x < 0. then
    let a, b = parts (-. x) in
      (-. a, b)
    else
      (floor x, x -. floor x)
```

Notice that we are using the unary operator `-.` to make the number positive.

4

We need to determine at which column the asterisk will be printed. It is important to make sure that the range 0 . . . 1 is split into fifty equal sized parts, which requires some careful thought. Then, we just print enough spaces to pad the line, add the asterisk, and a newline character.

```
star : float → unit

let star x =
  let i = int_of_float (floor (x *. 50.)) in
    let i' = if i = 50 then 49 else i in
      for x = 1 to i' - 1 do print_char ' ' done;
      print_char '*';
      print_newline ()
```

5

We use a reference to hold the current value, starting at the beginning of the range, and then loop until we are outside the range.

```
plot : (float → float) → float → float → float → unit

let plot f a b dy =
  let pos = ref a in
    while !pos <= b do
      star (f !pos);
      pos := !pos +. dy
    done
```

No allowance has been made here for bad arguments (for example, b smaller than a). Can you extend our program to move the zero-point to the middle of the screen, so that the sine function can be graphed even when its result is less than zero?

Chapter 15 (The OCaml Standard Library)

1

A non-tail-recursive one is simple:

```
concat : α list list → α list

let rec concat l =
  match l with
    [] -> []
  | h::t -> h @ concat t
```

To make a tail-recursive one, we can use an accumulator, reversing each list as we append it, and reversing the result. List.rev is tail-recursive already.

```
concat_tail : α list → α list list → α list
concat : α list list → α list

let rec concat_tail a l =
  match l with
    [] -> List.rev a
  | h::t -> concat_tail (List.rev h @ a) t

let concat l =
  concat_tail [] l
```

2

We can use `List.mem`, partially applied, to map over the list of lists. We then make sure that `false` is not in the resultant list, again with `List.mem`.

```
all_contain_true : bool list list → bool

let all_contain_true l =
  not (List.mem false (List.map (List.mem true) l))
```

3

The `String.iter` function calls a user-supplied function of type **char** → **unit** on each character of the string. We can use this to increment a counter when an exclamation mark is found.

```
count_exclamations : string → int

let count_exclamations s =
  let n = ref 0 in
    String.iter (function '!' -> n := !n + 1 | _ -> ()) s;
    !n
```

The contents of the counter is then the result of the function.

4

We can use the `String.map` function, which takes a user-supplied function of type **char** → **char** and returns a new string, where each character is the result of the mapping function on the character in the same place in the old string.

```
calm : string → string

let calm =
  String.map (function '!' -> '.' | x -> x)
```

Notice that we have taken advantage of partial application to erase the last argument as usual.

5

Looking at the documentation for the `String` module we find the following:

```
val concat : string -> string list -> string

    String.concat sep sl concatenates the list of strings sl, inserting the sepa-
    rator string sep between each.
```

So, by using the empty string as a separator, we have what we want:

```
concat: string list → string

let concat =
  String.concat ""
```

6

We can use the functions `create`, `add_string`, and `contents` from the `Buffer` module together with the usual list iterator `List.iter`:

```
concat : string list → string

let concat ss =
  let b = Buffer.create 100 in
    List.iter (Buffer.add_string b) ss;
    Buffer.contents b
```

The initial size of the buffer, 100, is arbitrary.

7

We repeatedly check if the string we are looking for is right at the beginning of the string to be searched. If not, we chop one character off the string to be searched, and try again. Every time we find a match, we increment a counter.

```
occurrences : string → string → int

let occurrences ss s =                          occurrences of ss in s
  if ss = "" then 0 else                            defined as zero
    let num = ref 0 in                       occurrences found so far
      let str = ref s in                            current string
        while
          String.length ss <= String.length !str && !str <> ""
        do
          if String.sub !str 0 (String.length ss) = ss then
            num := !num + 1;
          str := String.sub !str 1 (String.length !str - 1)
        done;
        !num
```

You might consider that writing this function with lists of characters rather than strings would be easier. Unfortunately, it would be slow, and these kinds of searching tasks are often required to be very fast.

Chapter 16 (Building Bigger Programs)

1

First, we extend the Textstat module to allow frequencies to be counted and expose it through the interface, shown in Figures 16.6 and 16.7. Then the main program is as shown in Figure 16.8.

2

We can write two little functions – one to read all the lines from a file, and one to write them. The main function, then, reads the command line to find the input and output file names, reads the lines from the input, reverses the list of lines, and writes them out. If a problem occurs, the exception is printed out. If the command line is badly formed, we print a usage message and exit. This is shown in Figure 16.9.

Note that there is a problem if the file has no final newline – it will end up with one. How might you solve that?

3

We can simply do something (or nothing) a huge number of times using a **for** loop.

```
(* A program which takes sufficiently long to run that we can distinguish
between the ocamlc and ocamlopt compilers *)

for x = 1 to 10000000 do
  ()
done
```

On many systems, typing time followed by a space and the usual command will print out on the screen how long the program took to run. For example, on the author's computer:

```
type stats

val lines : stats -> int

val characters : stats -> int

val words : stats -> int

val sentences : stats -> int

val frequency : stats -> char -> int

val stats_from_file : string -> stats
```

Figure 16.6: `textstat.mli`

```
$ ocamlc bigloop.ml -o bigloop
$ time ./bigloop

real  0m1.896s
user  0m1.885s
sys   0m0.005s

$ ocamlopt bigloop.ml -o bigloop
$ time ./bigloop

real  0m0.022s
user  0m0.014s
sys   0m0.003s
```

You can see that, when compiled with `ocamlc`, it takes 1.9s to run, but when compiled with `ocamlopt` just
0.022s.

4

We can get all the lines in the file using our `getlines` function from question two. The main function
simply calls `string_in_line` on each line, printing it if `true` is returned.

The interesting function is `string_in_line`. To see if `term` is in `line` we start at position 0. The
condition for the term having been found is a combination of boolean expressions. The first ensures that
we are not so far through the string that the expression could not possibly fit at the current position. The
second checks to see if the term is found at the current position by using the function `String.sub` from
the OCaml Standard Library. If not, we carry on. This is illustrated in Figure 16.10.

```
(* Text statistics *)
type stats = int * int * int * int * int array

(* Utility functions to retrieve parts of a stats value *)
let lines (l, _, _, _, _) = l

let characters (_, c, _, _, _) = c

let words (_, _, w, _, _) = w

let sentences (_, _, _, s, _) = s

let frequency (_, _, _, _, h) x = h.(int_of_char x)

(* Read statistics from a channel *)
let stats_from_channel in_channel =
  let lines = ref 0 in
  let characters = ref 0 in
  let words = ref 0 in
  let sentences = ref 0 in
  let histogram = Array.make 256 0 in
    try
      while true do
        let line = input_line in_channel in
          lines := !lines + 1;
          characters := !characters + String.length line;
          String.iter
            (fun c ->
              match c with
              '.' | '?' | '!' -> sentences := !sentences + 1
            | ' ' -> words := !words + 1
            | _ -> ())
            line;
          String.iter
            (fun c ->
              let i = int_of_char c in
                histogram.(i) <- histogram.(i) + 1)
            line
      done;
      (0, 0, 0, 0, [||]) (* Just to make the type agree *)
    with
      End_of_file -> (!lines, !characters, !words, !sentences, histogram)

(* Read statistics, given a filename. Exceptions are not handled *)
let stats_from_file filename =
  let channel = open_in filename in
    let result = stats_from_channel channel in
      close_in channel;
      result
```

Figure 16.7: textstat.ml

```ocaml
let print_histogram stats =
  print_string "Character frequencies:\n";
  for x = 0 to 255 do
    let freq = Textstat.frequency stats (char_of_int x) in
      if freq > 0 then
        begin
          print_string "For character '";
          print_char (char_of_int x);
          print_string "' (character number ";
          print_int x;
          print_string ") the count is ";
          print_int freq;
          print_string ".\n"
        end
      done
in
  try
    begin match Sys.argv with
      [|_; filename|] ->
        let stats = Textstat.stats_from_file filename in
          print_string "Words: ";
          print_int (Textstat.words stats);
          print_newline ();
          print_string "Characters: ";
          print_int (Textstat.characters stats);
          print_newline ();
          print_string "Sentences: ";
          print_int (Textstat.sentences stats);
          print_newline ();
          print_string "Lines: ";
          print_int (Textstat.lines stats);
          print_newline ();
          print_histogram stats
    | _ ->
        print_string "Usage: stats <filename>\n"
    end
  with
    e ->
      print_string "An error occurred: ";
      print_string (Printexc.to_string e);
      print_newline ();
      exit 1
```

Figure 16.8: stats.ml

```
(* Reverse the lines in a file *)

let putlines lines filename =
  let channel = open_out filename in
    List.iter
      (fun s ->
         output_string channel s;
         output_char channel '\n')
      lines;
    close_out channel

let getlines filename =
  let channel = open_in filename in
    let lines = ref [] in
      try
        while true do
          lines := input_line channel :: !lines
        done;
        []
      with
        End_of_file ->
          close_in channel;
          List.rev !lines

let _ =
  match Sys.argv with
    [|_; infile; outfile|] ->
      begin
        try
          let lines = List.rev (getlines infile) in
            putlines lines outfile
        with
          e ->
            print_string "There was an error. Details follow:\n";
            print_string (Printexc.to_string e);
            print_newline ();
            exit 1
      end
  | _ ->
      print_string "Usage: reverse input_filename output_filename\n";
      exit 1
```

Figure 16.9: reverse.ml

```
let rec string_in_line term line pos =
    pos + String.length term <= String.length line
  &&
    (String.sub line pos (String.length term) = term
    || string_in_line term line (pos + 1))

let getlines filename =
  let channel = open_in filename in
    let lines = ref [] in
      try
        while true do
          lines := input_line channel :: !lines
        done;
        []
      with
        End_of_file ->
          close_in channel;
          List.rev !lines

let _ =
  match Sys.argv with
    [|_; searchterm; filename|] ->
      begin
        try
          List.iter
            (fun line ->
                if string_in_line searchterm line 0 then
                  begin
                    print_string line;
                    print_newline ()
                  end)
            (getlines filename)
        with
          e ->
            print_string "An error occurred:\n";
            print_string (Printexc.to_string e);
            print_newline ()
      end
  | _ ->
    print_string "Usage: search search_term filename\n"
```

Figure 16.10: `search.ml`

Hints for Questions

Chapter 1
Starting Off

1

Try to work these out on paper, and then check by typing them in. Remember that the type of an expression is the type of the value it will evaluate to. Can you show the steps of evaluation for each expression?

2

Type each expression in. What number does each evaluate to? Can you work out which operator (mod or +) is being calculated first?

3

Type it in. What does OCaml print? What is the evaluation order?

7

What if a value of 2 appeared? How might we interpret it?

Chapter 2
Names and Functions

1

The function takes one integer, and returns that integer multiplied by ten. So what must its type be?

2

What does the function take as arguments? What is the type of its result? So what is the whole type? You can use the <> and && operators here.

3

This will be a recursive function, so remember to use **let rec**. What is the sum of all the integers from 1 . . . 1? Perhaps this is a good base case.

4

This will be a recursive function. What happens when you raise a number to the power 0? What about the power 1? What about a higher power?

5

Can you define this in terms of the isvowel function we have already written?

6

Try adding parentheses to the expression in a way which does not change its meaning. Does this make it easier to understand?

7

When does it not terminate? Can you add a check to see when it might happen, and return 0 instead? What is the factorial of 0 anyway?

Chapter 3
Case by Case

1

We are pattern matching on a boolean value, so there are just two cases: `true` and `false`.

2

Convert the **if ... then ... else** structure of the `sum` function from the previous chapter into a pattern matching structure.

3

You will need three cases as before – when the power is 0, 1 or greater than 1 – but now in the form of a pattern match.

5

Consider where parentheses might be added without altering the expression.

6

There will be two cases in each function – the special range pattern x..y, and _ for any other character.

Chapter 4
Making Lists

1

Consider three cases: (1) the argument list is empty, (2) the argument list has one element, (3) the argument list has more than one element a::b::t. In the last case, which element do we need to miss out?

2

The function will have type **bool list→ int**. Consider the empty list, the list with `true` as its head, and the list with `false` as its head. Count one for each `true` and zero for each `false`.

3

The function to make a palindrome is trivial; to detect if a list is a palindrome, consider the definition of a palindrome – a list which equals its own reverse.

4

Consider the cases (1) the empty list, (2) the list with one element, and (3) the list with more than one element. For the tail recursive version, use an accumulating argument.

5

Can any element exist in the empty list? If the list is not empty, it must have a head and a tail. What is the answer if the element we are looking for is equal to the head? What do we do if it is not?

6

The empty list is already a set. If we have a head and a tail, what does it tell us to find out if the head exists within the tail?

7

Consider in which order the @ operators are evaluated in the reverse function. How long does each append take? How many are there?

Chapter 5
Sorting Things

1

Consider adding another **let** before **let** left and **let** right.

2

Consider the situations in which `take` and `drop` can fail, and what arguments `msort` gives them at each recursion.

3

This is a simple change – consider the comparison operator itself.

4

What will the type of the function be? Lists of length zero and one are already sorted – so these will be the base cases. What do we do when there is more than one element?

6

You can put one **let rec** construct inside another.

Chapter 6
Functions upon Functions upon Functions

1

The function `calm` is simple recursion on lists. There are three cases – the empty list, a list beginning with `'!'` and a list beginning with any other character. In the second part of the question, write a function `calm_char` which processes a single character. You can then use `map` to define a new version of `calm`.

2

This is the same process as Question 1.

3

Look back at the section on anonymous functions. How can `clip` be expressed as an anonymous function? So, how can we use it with `map`?

4

We want a function of the form **let rec** `apply f n x = ...` which applies f to x a total of n times. What is the base case? What do we do in that case? What otherwise?

5

You will need to add the extra function as an argument to both `insert` and `sort` and use it in place of the `<=` operator in `insert`.

6

There are three possibilities: the argument list is empty, `true` is returned when its head is given to the function f, or `false` is returned when its head is given to the function f.

7

If the input list is empty, the result is trivially true – there cannot possibly be any elements for which the function does not hold. If not, it must hold for the first one, and for all the others by recursion.

8

You can use `map` on each α **list** in the α **list list**.

Chapter 7
When Things Go Wrong

1

Make sure to consider the case of the empty list, where there is no smallest positive element, and also the non-empty list containing entirely zero or negative numbers.

2

Just put an exception handler around the function in the previous question.

3

First, write a function to find the number less than or equal to the square root of its argument. Now, define a suitable exception, and wrap up your function in another which, on a bad argument, raises the exception or otherwise calls your first function.

4

Use the **try** ... **with** construct to call your function and handle the exception you defined.

Chapter 8
Looking Things Up

1

The keys in a dictionary are unique – does remembering that fact help you?

2

The type will be the same as for the **add** function, but we only replace something if we find it there – when do we know we will not find it?

3

The function takes a list of keys and a list of values, and returns a dictionary. So it will have type α **list** $\rightarrow \beta$ **list** $\rightarrow (\alpha \times \beta)$ **list**. Try matching on both lists at once – what are the cases?

4

This function takes a list of pairs and produces a pair of lists. So its type must be $(\alpha \times \beta)$ **list** $\rightarrow \alpha$ **list** $\times \beta$ **list**.

For the base case (the empty dictionary), we can see that the result should be ([], []). But what to do in the case we have (k, v) :: more? We must get names for the two parts of the result of our function on more, and then cons k and v on to them – can you think of how to do that?

5

You can keep a list of the keys which have already been seen, and use the **member** function to make sure you do not add to the result list a key-value pair whose key has already been included.

6

The function will take two dictionaries, and return another – so you should be able to write down its type easily.

Try pattern matching on the first list – when it is empty, the answer is trivial – what about when it has a head and a tail?

Chapter 9
More with Functions

2

Try building a list of booleans, each representing the result of **member** on a list.

3

The / operator differs from the ∗ operator in an important sense. What is it?

4

The type of map is $(\alpha \rightarrow \beta) \rightarrow \alpha$ **list** $\rightarrow \beta$ **list**. The type of mapl is $(\alpha \rightarrow \beta) \rightarrow \alpha$ **list list** $\rightarrow \beta$ **list list**. So, what must the type of mapll be? Now, look at our definition of mapl – how can we extend it to lists of lists of lists?

5

Use our revised **take** function to process a single list. You may then use **map** with this (partially applied) function to build the **truncate** function.

6

Build a function **firstelt** which, given the number and a list, returns the first element or that number. You can then use this function (partially applied) together with **map** to build the main **firstelts** function.

Chapter 10
New Kinds of Data

1

The type will have two constructors: one for squares, requiring only a single integer, and one for rectangles, requiring two: one for the width and one for the height.

2

The function will have type rect → **int**. Work by pattern matching on the two constructors of your type.

3

Work by pattern matching on your type. What happens to a square. What to a rectangle?

4

First, we need to rotate the rectangles as needed – you have already written something for this. Then, we need to sort them according to width. Can you use our sort function which takes a custom comparison function for this?

5

Look at how we re-wrote length and append for the sequence type.

6

Add another constructor, and amend evaluate as necessary.

7

Handle the exception, and return None in that case.

Chapter 11
Growing Trees

1

The type will be $\alpha \rightarrow \alpha$ tree $\rightarrow$ **bool**. That is, it takes an element to search for, and a tree containing elements of the same type, and returns true if the element is found, and false if not. What happens if the tree is a leaf? What if it is a branch?

2

The function will have type α tree $\rightarrow \alpha$ tree. What happens to a leaf? What must happen to a branch and its sub-trees?

3

If the two trees are both Lf, they have the same shape. What if they are both branches? What if one is a branch and the other a leaf or vice versa? For the second part of the question, consider a devious way to use map_tree to produce trees of like type.

4

We have already written a function for inserting an element into an existing tree.

5

Try using list dictionaries as an intermediate representation. We already know how to build a tree from a list.

6

Consider using a list of sub-trees for a branch. How can we represent a branch which has no sub-trees?

Chapter 12
In and Out

1

You can use the print_string and print_int functions. Be careful about what happens when you print the last number.

2

You can use the `read_int` function to read an integer from the user. Be sure to give the user proper instructions, and to deal with the case where `read_int` raises an exception (which it will if the user does not type an integer).

3

One way would be to ask the user how many dictionary entries they intend to type in first. Then we do not need a special code to signal the end of input.

4

Try writing a function to build a list of integers from 1 to n. Can you use that to build the table and print it? The `iter` and/or `map` functions may come in useful. Deal with a channel in your innermost function – the opening and closing of the file can be dealt with elsewhere.

5

The `input_line` function can be used – how many times can you call it until `End_of_file` is raised?

6

We can read lines from the file using `input_line` and write using `output_string` – make sure the newlines do not get lost! How do we know when we are done? Write a function to copy a line from one channel to another – we can deal with opening and closing the files separately.

Chapter 13
Putting Things in Boxes

1

Consider the initial values of the references, and then work through how each one is altered by each part of the expression. What is finally returned as the result of the expression?

2

Try creating a value for each list in OCaml. Now try getting the head of the list, which is a reference, and updating its contents to another integer. What has happened in each case?

3

Try writing a function `forloop` which takes a function to be applied to each number, and the start and end numbers. It should call the given function on each number. What should happen when the start number is larger than the end number?

4

Type them in if you are stuck. Can you work out why each expression has the type OCaml prints?

5

We want a function of type **int array** $\rightarrow$ **int**. Try a for loop with a reference to accumulate the sum.

6

Consider swapping elements from opposite ends of the array – the problem is symmetric.

7

To build an array of arrays, you will need a use `Array.make` to build an array of empty arrays. You can then set each of the elements of the main array to a suitably sized array, again created with `Array.make`. Once the structure is in place, putting the numbers in should be simple.

8

What is the difference between the codes for `'a'` and `'A'`? What about `'z'` and `'Z'`?

Chapter 14
The Other Numbers

1

Consider the built-in functions `ceil` and `floor`.

2

This is simple arithmetic. The function will take two points and return another, so it will have type **float** × **float** → **float** × **float** → **float** × **float**.

3

Consider the built-in function `floor`. What should happen in the case of a negative number?

4

Calculate the column number for the asterisk carefully. How can it be printed in the correct column?

5

You will need to call the `star` function with an appropriate argument at points between the beginning and end of the range, as determined by the step.

Chapter 15
The OCaml Standard Library

1

You can assume `List.rev` which is tail-recursive.

2

You might use `List.map` here, together with `List.mem`

3

The `String.iter` function should help here.

4

Try `String.map` supplying a suitable function.

5

Consider `String.concat`.

6

Create a buffer, add all the strings to it in order, and then return its contents.

7

`String.sub` is useful here. You can compare strings with one another for equality, as with any other type.

Chapter 16
Building Bigger Programs

1

You will need to alter the `Textstat` module to calculate the histogram and allow it to be accessed through the module's interface. Then, alter the main program to retrieve and print the extra information.

2

You will need functions to read and write the lines. You can read the required input and output filenames from `Sys.argv`. What should we do in case of an error, e.g. a bad filename?

3

Consider doing something a very large number of times. You should avoid printing information to the screen, because the printing speed might dominate, and the differing computation speeds may be hard to notice.

4

Start with a function to search for a given string inside another. You might find some functions from the `String` module in the OCaml Standard Library to be useful, or you can write it from first principles. Once this is done, the rest is simple.

Coping with Errors

It is very hard to write even small programs correctly the first time. An unfortunate but inevitable part of programming is the location and fixing of mistakes. OCaml has a range of messages to help you with this process.

Here are descriptions of the common messages OCaml prints when a program cannot be accepted or when running it causes a problem (a so-called "run-time error"). We also describe warnings OCaml prints to alert the programmer to a program which, though it can be accepted for evaluation, might contain mistakes.

ERRORS

These are messages printed when an expression could not be accepted for evaluation, due to being malformed in some way. No evaluation is attempted. You must fix the expression and try again.

Syntax error

This error occurs when OCaml finds that the program text contains things which are not valid words (such as **if**, **let** etc.) or other basic parts of the language, or when they exist in invalid combinations – this is known as *syntax*. Check carefully and try again.

```
OCaml
```

```
#1 +;;
Error: syntax error
```

OCaml has underlined where it thinks the error is. Since this error occurs for a wide range of different mistakes and problems, the underlining may not pinpoint the exact position of your mistake.

Unbound value ...

This error occurs when you have mentioned a name which has not been defined (technically "bound to a value"). This might happen if you have mistyped the name.

```
OCaml
```

```
# x + 1;;
Error: Unbound value x
```

In our example x is not defined, so it has been underlined.

This expression has type ... but an expression was expected of type ...

You will see this error very frequently. It occurs when the expression's syntax is correct (i.e. it is made up of valid words and constructs), and OCaml has moved on to type-checking the expression prior to evaluation. If there is a problem with type-checking, OCaml shows you where a mismatch between the expected and actual type occurred.

```
        OCaml
```

```
# 1 + true;;
Error: This expression has type bool but an expression was expected of type
       int
```

In this example, OCaml is looking for an integer on the right hand side of the + operator, and finds something of type **bool** instead.

It is not always as easy to spot the real source of the problem, especially if the function is recursive. Nevertheless, a careful look at the program will often shine light on the problem – look at each function and its arguments, and try to find your mistake.

This function is applied to too many arguments

Exactly what it says. The function name is underlined.

```
        OCaml
```

```
# let f x = x + 1;;
val f : int -> int = <fun>
# f x y;;
Error: This function is applied to too many arguments;
maybe you forgot a `;'
```

The phrase "maybe you forgot a ';' " applies to imperative programs where accidently missing out a ';' between successive function applications might commonly lead to this error.

Unbound constructor ...

This occurs when a constructor name is used which is not defined.

```
        OCaml
```

```
# type t = Roof | Wall | Floor;;
type t = Roof | Wall | Floor
# Window;;
Error: Unbound constructor Window
```

OCaml knows it is a constructor name because it has an initial capital letter.

The constructor ... expects ... argument(s), but is applied here to ... argument(s)

This error occurs when the wrong kind of data is given to a constructor for a type. It is just another type error, but we get a specialised message.

OCaml

```
# type p = A of int | B of bool;;
type p = A of int | B of bool
# A;;
Error: The constructor A expects 1 argument(s),
       but is applied here to 0 argument(s)
```

RUN-TIME ERRORS

In any programming language powerful enough to be of use, some errors cannot be detected before attempting evaluation of an expression (until "run-time"). The exception mechanism is for handling and recovering from these kinds of problems.

Stack overflow during evaluation (looping recursion?)

This occurs if the function builds up a working expression which is too big. This might occur if the function is never going to stop because of a programming error, or if the argument is just too big.

OCaml

```
# let rec f x = 1 + f (x + 1);;
val f : int -> int = <fun>
# f 0;;
Stack overflow during evaluation (looping recursion?).
```

Find the cause of the unbounded recursion, and try again. If it is really not a mistake, rewrite the function to use an accumulating argument (and so, to be tail recursive).

Exception: Match_failure ...

This occurs when a pattern match cannot find anything to match against. You would have been warned about this possibility when the program was originally entered. For example, if the following function f were defined as

```
let f x = match x with 0 -> 1
```

then using the function with 1 as an argument would produce:

OCaml

```
# f 1;;
Exception: Match_failure ("//toplevel//", 1, 10).
```

In this example, the match failure occurred in the top level (i.e. the interactive OCaml we are using), at line one, character ten.

Exception: ...

This is printed if an un-handled exception reaches OCaml.

OCaml

```
# exception Exp of string;;
exception Exp of string
# raise (Exp "Failed");;
Exception: Exp "Failed".
```

This can occur for built-in exceptions like Division_by_Zero or Not_found or ones the user has defined like Exp above.

WARNINGS

Warnings do not stop an expression being accepted or evaluated. They are printed after an expression is accepted but before the expression is evaluated. Warnings are for occasions where OCaml is concerned you may have made a mistake, even though the expression is not actually malformed. You should check each new warning in a program carefully.

This pattern-matching is not exhaustive

This warning is printed when OCaml has determined that you have missed out one or more cases in a pattern match. This could result in a Match_failure exception being raised at run-time.

OCaml

```
# let f x = match x with 0 -> 1;;
Warning 8: this pattern-matching is not exhaustive.
Here is an example of a value that is not matched:
1
val f : int -> int = <fun>
```

Helpfully, it is able to generate an example of something the pattern match does not cover, so this should give you a hint about what has been missed out. You may ignore the warning if you are sure that, for other reasons, this case can never occur.

This match case is unused

This occurs when two parts of the pattern match cover the same case. In this situation, the second one could never be reached, so it is almost certain the programmer has made a mistake.

```
        OCaml
```

```
# let f x = match x with _ -> 1 | 0 -> 0;;
Warning 11: this match case is unused.
val f : int -> int = <fun>
```

In this case, the first case matches everything, so the second cannot ever match.

This expression should have type unit

Sometimes when writing imperative programs, we ignore the result of some side-effect-producing function. However, this can indicate a mistake.

```
        OCaml
```

```
# f 1; 2;;
Warning 10: this expression should have type unit.
- : int = 2
```

It is better to use the built-in ignore function in these cases, to avoid this warning:

```
        OCaml
```

```
# ignore (f 1); 2;;
- : int = 2
```

The ignore function has type $\alpha \rightarrow$ **unit**. It has no side-effect.

Index

Printed in Great Britain
by Amazon